D0971762

HOW TO PITCH & SELL YOUR TV SCRIPT

HOW TO
PITCH & SELL
YOUR
TV SCRIPT

D A V I D   S I L V E R

Writer's
Digest
Books

Cincinnati, Ohio

95 94 93 92 91   5 4 3 2 1

Library of Congress Cataloging in Publication Data

Silver, David.
    How to pitch and sell your TV script / by David Silver. — 1st ed.
        p.   cm.
    Includes index.
    ISBN 0-89879-467-6 (hard-cover)
    1. Television authorship — Marketing.   I. Title.
PN1992.7.S55   1991
808.2-25-0688 — dc20   91-2697
                                                                     CIP

Edited by Bob Korth
Designed by Sandy Conopeotis

To Sarah, Sandra and Victor

My sincere thanks go to Frank Coffey for guiding me through this process; Les Koch for getting me involved in the first place; Morris Neuman for enduring my primitive software queries; and to Terri Boemker, Marilyn and Steve Bosworth, Don Condra, Fran DeFeo, Nan Dibble, Robert Drescher, Ali Gertz, Bob Korth, Bruce Ligerman, Kate Morrow, Lynn Perrigo, Janine Ranieri, Robert Rosenblatt, Brian Siberell, Sequoyah Silver, Ronni Simon, Tim Snow, Calliope Thorne and Stu Werbin.

TABLE OF CONTENTS

Chapter One:

WHAT EXACTLY IS WRITING FOR TELEVISION?

YOU WATCH TELEVISION AND YOU SAY TO YOURSELF: "I'M A writer. I could do so much better than that. . . . I'm going to do it! Write a film, a sitcom, a documentary . . . why not?" Why not, indeed? There's no huge mystical reason why any writer shouldn't be able to put together a decent film. Why shouldn't it be you?

The Essence of the Genre

Television is a visual medium, yet the written word is the essential building block behind almost the whole industry. News stories are just that—"stories." Sitcoms are based on written banter and jokes; dramatic series and movies-of-the-week are written dialogue; documentaries are given coherence by the carefully written "voice-over"; even the Johnny Carson, David Letterman, and Arsenio Hall shows are created by highly paid teams of writers. TV is a writer's medium, no doubt about it.

But if you have written for other media, clearly understand that you are entering new genres with new disciplines attached. Sure, a short story or a novel can be adapted into a teleplay, an article into a documentary, but you need to think seriously about how to train yourself to write for a visual product. It helps if you have written advertising copy, but even then, there is a vast difference between writing short, pithy thirty-second spots and putting together a long-form, coherent, compelling teleplay.

Where Do You Fit In?

This is the question that must be addressed before any of the necessary machinations start. To answer this requires a mixture of instinct and intelligence. Your heart (or maybe your stomach) should tell you what to write and for whom.

If you are imaginative, constantly coming up with dramatic situations in your head, the fiction/drama route is obvious. Breaking that route down further, do you have extended "plot" thoughts, dreams and daydreams, or are they short, funny visions that would fit the situation comedy genre?

Although you may not fit tightly into any one of these categories exclusively, people usually do, at least at the start. Are you committed to various causes and social ideas, and are you an especially observant person, routinely thinking about the state of society? If this is the case, even though you may also want to dramatize these concepts, you would be well advised to think about documentaries and news.

Before you contact anyone or even write anything, you must look inside yourself to find the exact place for you in the medium. If you cannot answer these questions, then write anyway and monitor exactly what you are writing. Soon, you will clearly see where you should be aiming. After all, creative writing does not emerge out of a machine but out of a combination of mind and heart. You feel something, you think something about that feeling, and then you put pen to paper or fingertips to typewriter (or word processor).

Tricks of the Trade

In the 1980s, markets for TV- and filmwriters expanded dramatically — home video and cable television, plus the increasing interest of foreign outlets, created a situation in which writers could find many more places to submit material.

But how does a writer penetrate these markets? What are the essential, correct "methods of operation" to be successful in this exciting field? Undeniably there are discouraging factors that can stop you from a decision to actually do it. How do you break into the whole scene? Who do you contact? How do you express what you have inside your head, and how do you make "them" listen? Is it all nepotism and connections made at fancy parties? Do you need a powerful agent, and how in heaven's name do you get one? Do you live in the right place—*is* there a "right place"? Do professional TV writers have something that you just do not have?

There are no absolute rules, and serendipity plays its role as always, but I have learned after over twenty years of involvement in this process that there are definite guidelines that will help you get your ideas financed and produced.

Even if an idea or script is strong and original, we are living in a complex, institutionalized media environment, and it is imperative that neophyte writers learn some tricks of the trade to get their property sold and made. You must learn how to communicate with the communicators; you must be as ingenious in your presentation as in your imagination. That is the essence of this book.

Why Read This Book?

Writing is an art, but getting it developed and produced is more like a science. There are proven ways to succeed, and this book is a distillation of them based on my own and other professionals' experience.

This book gives you clear, relatively simple ways to put yourself through the basic training needed to convert ideas into successful scripts and proposals. More precisely, it gives you the wherewithal to get these ideas across in the most appropriate way. No one can give you the gift of creativity, but this book, based on experience, can make you effective in the marketplace. The process is not as tough as that of the Marine Corps, but it is rigorous and requires perseverance and dedication. The path is one of strategy and clear thinking. In the following chapters, I lead you through the process, from putting your material down on paper to making the final presentation. There is detailed discussion of agents, story editors, producers, production companies, networks, how to call on the phone (both "cold" and with a contact), how to make the most of your meetings, proposal writing, treatments, teleplays, outlines and the rest. I also venture some simple psychology, based on my personal experience, on the subject of maintaining confidence and élan in the face of rejection and delay, two staples of the television writing game. In every way, I will put you further down the line than I was when I started submitting material—I had no practical guidebooks to consult at that time. It helps to reap the benefits of someone else's experience, particularly when that writer has experienced most of the reactions in the professional spectrum.

Your idea is your own, and no one can write it for you, but there are many time-tested methods of making the most of your creative ability. Television in particular is a field where precedent, professional etiquette and patience are a crucial part of the progress of the writer. After many years of dealing with TV executives and producers of all kinds, I can say that if the idea is a good one and you show that you can write, there is usually some positive response to your work. It may not get accepted immediately—this very rarely happens. It is essentially a slow building process, but if you can write and are prepared to keep pushing and waiting and pushing and waiting, there will be success at the end of the line. It sometimes takes weeks, sometimes years, but if you truly want to be a professional television writer, there is almost always a place for you in the industry.

Chapter Two:

WHAT

A

WRITER

NEEDS

AFTER BECOMING WELL AWARE OF WHAT IS ACTUALLY ON TELE-vision, the kind of fare that actually gets produced and broadcast, you are ready to engage in some sensible self-analysis in order to fit yourself into the picture.

A Little Self-Analysis

Decide on what captivates you as a writer. If social issues like alcoholism, abuse, crime, relationships or politics grab you, decide whether you want to create something dramatic or whether you would prefer a documentary. If it is a completely inspired idea that does not fit into any neat category, track it down in your mind and write notes about what compels you.

The key initial factor is the quality of your work. No matter how brilliantly you engineer routes to TV writing success, not much will happen (in the vast majority of cases) unless the written material is good, if not outstanding. The strength of the original idea, the explanation of this idea, and the eventual execution are of paramount importance. It is almost impossible to persevere with a weak idea or a floundering exposition.

Before anyone else can possibly like your material, you have to like it—no, more than that, you have to *love* it. We have all read articles and seen television shows and movies where we immediately felt the passion of the writer, the accuracy of the detail, the importance of the information. And vice versa. Ultimately, you cannot fool anybody, most of all the wily, sometimes jaded agents, story editors and/or producers who will be the first, crucial filters through which your work will pass.

You must be completely enmeshed in your subject matter — be it dramatic or documentary — and this semiobsessive attitude must be maintained from the writing of the first documents to the presentation of the finished material. Otherwise, you are basically wasting your time.

Ability and Business Sense

If you have never written anything, it is important to find out whether you have some sort of natural ability to write. I would never dare to suggest that unless you have inbuilt talents, you should forget the whole thing. Many people have assiduously learned how to write. It is an easier path if you have an immediate flair for putting your thoughts down on paper. It helps even more if you are a writer who thinks visually without too much strain. But even this can be learned — it can be trained into you by a skilled teacher or by dogged practice.

It definitely helps to read about scriptwriting. You may want to start by reading one or more of these: Jurgen Wolff and Kerry Cox's *Successful Scriptwriting*, J. Michael Straczynski's *The Complete Book of Scriptwriting* (both Writer's Digest Books), Syd Field's *Screenplay: The Foundations of Screenwriting* (Dell) or Wells Root's *Writing the Script: A Practical Guide for Films and Television* (Holt, Rinehart and Winston). These four books, and a few others, will give you valuable information about where to start and how to feel confident about the actual writing.

Read books of teleplays and screenplays. Paddy Chayevsky's work from the early days of television still holds up, is top-notch, and is thoroughly enjoyable to boot. Watch TV movies or documentaries, depending on what you want to do. Be careful, though: Watching TV will give you only the polished final product and could misguide you. The initial stages aren't on the screen, and concentrating exclusively on the final product won't show you the way to get there.

Read about and watch TV. Become acquainted with the contours of actual shows and tricks to keep an audience watching. One of the most annoying and pretentious statements coming out of writers is that they don't watch television. You must study the medium to get a utilitarian sense of what writing gets on and what doesn't. Sometimes, certainly, you take a completely innovative approach and your work breaks through because it is obviously worthy, but even then you have to know basically what you are dealing with. In most cases, if you want a career for yourself in the mainstream of the business, you must know the range of programming out there and who is responsible for it.

Added to this—in order to have any tangible success in a thoroughly commercial field—you must have, or learn to have, good business sense right from the start. This entails self-organization, daily persistence and positive thinking.

The Right Perceptions

Never listen to people who say that TV is a medium for hacks, hustlers and has-beens. We know why they're saying things like that, but don't allow yourself to be poisoned by these jaded sermons. Everyone has put television down for years as awful and bad and corruptly influential—it can be all that—but it is also the medium of our age, and it is (and should be) utterly exciting for you when you get something produced and broadcast. If it is good and does not fall into the product of the "Three Aitches" (hacks, hustlers and has-beens), then you have ameliorated the condition of a massively influential medium and maybe, just maybe, you have spread some positive, useful information into the society and body politic. So the "TV stinks and so does your writing" rap must be banished before you do anything.

I believe that television has its own small band of inspired geniuses and also a veritable posse of highly skilled writers, so join the club with self-esteem. TV is better than it used to be, even better than it ever was, though at its most crass end it is also the worst it has ever been. So, given that you want to have your work produced, firmly view yourself as a positive addition to an improving field. Then your project will be the best it can be.

The Deep Rewards of Getting Work Produced

The business side is obviously important, but knowing there is real worth in what you do is even more important than money. There is huge satisfaction in creating something you believe in and knowing that it will reach millions of people. Think of it— most of that audience is individually very small: three people, often two people, often one person. These tiny coteries of watchers, if the show is good or great, can be deeply affected by what you have written.

Your work—the final, polished version of an artifact stretching all the way back to an early seed in your mind—is on the air, moving across the country, making people happy or sad or exhilarated, changing them in some way. This is where the success really starts: in the expectancy of this rush, this thrill—the joy and growth involved in getting something seriously produced.

Some years back I wrote, directed and produced a couple of unusual music specials for NBC Enterprises. Although this wasn't a writing gig, it was a very elaborate TV production, done at the highest level. When I was sitting in the trailer/control room outside a club on Fifty-seventh Street and Eleventh Avenue in New York City, looking at the monitors and seeing none other than Count Basie playing the piano, his band behind him and the unlikely person of Elvis Costello up front singing a Duke Ellington composition, I felt a terrific glow about it all.

Three months before, I was sitting in a conference room at NBC in Rockefeller Center and a very open-minded executive was asking me what would be a dream show involving the Count Basie Orchestra. Rather ridiculously, I came out with the idea of having Elvis Costello sing with the band. No one in the room (eight people) knew who Costello was; maybe they thought that I wanted the late Elvis Presley to do the gig and that I had lost my mind. Using a combination of patience and good old English charm, I persuaded them to go through with the idea.

The fulfillment of that crazy concept and the eventual sale of the product to pay-per-view cable TV were very satisfying to me. It was the kind of feeling you always get when something is sold and actually produced. And this cuts through all the variables of TV creating. Seeing Elvis Costello sing with Basie, knowing that it wouldn't have happened without my exact ideation and execution, was a great spur for more work. Once you've seen one thing actualized, it pushes you on to greater things. Creating for television involves getting onto a continuum that, unless you are an employee of some kind of TV entity, requires an assiduous, stick-to-it stubbornness to keep you involved in the medium and enjoying the experience.

Questions for the Writer

If you are going to write for nonfiction television, then the word "focus" is paramount. The well-designed proposal, which I will cover in detail in a later chapter, is the key to the gold.

Again I must stress that, even if you are the slickest proposal writer on the planet, you must have real, abiding interest in and knowledge of your primary subject matter. In the documentary field, you are going after either independent backing or institutional money from entities such as the National Endowment for the Arts or the Rockefeller Foundation. These folks receive thousands of proposals every year and have a keen eye for what is real and what is not.

If you perceive yourself as primarily a nonfiction writer or writer/producer, you can travel several routes to become involved in the television industry, but if you are sufficiently confident to actually pitch your own ideas, trust your visceral feelings about what turns you on and which approach is the best one to take. Also, ask yourself before you attempt to get something produced: Has this been done before? The answer may be yes, but with the caveat that it hasn't been done *this way* before. Once you see that this project could be produced and distributed, then it is worthwhile embarking on the exciting, if arduous, journey toward production.

With fictional work, the main questions to ask before you decide to show it to the people who matter are: Can I truly see this

story? Is the essence of it already in my mind? Is it compelling?
Is it in some way commercial?

P's and Q's for the Writer

Passion is the fuel for all writing, whether for TV, movies, magazines or flyers on the street. Without this emotional commitment,
nothing will survive the long process of creation, production and
distribution. Even a TV situation comedy, which might appear
to lack passion in itself, has to have been formed by long hours
of work, alone and in committee and conference; not even the
most humdrum episode of "Growing Pains" or "Murphy Brown"
can be made without the passionate work attitudes of its creators.

I cannot think of a profession that requires more persistence
than that of writing for television. To break in takes enormous,
consistent pushing; to maintain takes even more. And the writing
itself always, without exception, requires the daily cultivation of
fresh energy and the actual pressing of typewriter or computer
keys. Nothing gets written without actual writing. When the con-
templation of the idea ends and the note-taking and research is
over, then the writing begins.

Persistence is probably the key to getting your writing and ideas
on the air. Unless you are basically unsuited to this whole vocation, the doors to success usually open when you learn how to
make yourself professionalize: You must institutionalize your
methods of pitching by developing a consistent approach to making phone calls, writing letters, and studying your craft. Plus regular writing. Persistence creates a long, hard, almost imperceiv-
able miracle. After a huge amount of persistence — a long period of
staying with it and maintaining a positive attitude throughout —
"sudden" success occurs almost organically.

Practicality is the third and most menacing of the P's, perhaps
because it is the most mundane. It forces you to maintain a realistic attitude toward the task at hand. What is the truth of the
situation? Can this work be sold to television? Budgeting, com-
merciality and topicality are all part of practicality, as is the clear
sense of whether this piece of yours is worth spending many
hours finishing, polishing and selling. Practicality also implies

being honest with yourself about the speed at which everything takes place. You may get positive feedback, even the suggestion of a buy or acquisition, but pre-production schedules often introduce surreal delays based on everything from sponsorship to politics to total irrationality. Being realistic cushions you from shocks, and blunts impatience and nervousness. A mellower attitude after a practical look at the real ball park involved brings about better productivity and a more secure, less pressured feeling on the part of those you are pitching to. It is never wasted energy to empathize with your buyers. Try your best to understand what they really want and what their limitations are—then you will create a product and an atmosphere that will more likely bring success.

Now, the three Q's—*quality*, *quantity*, and *quintessence*. Make sure that you are pitching the best thing that you have in its best, most completely "edited" version (quality).

Remember that the more good stuff you show—sometimes a whole script or a detailed proposal—the better it is (quantity). Admittedly, the pithy, condensed presentation is sometimes perfectly appropriate, but it makes sense, at least when you are starting out, to demonstrate as much of your writing and conceptual prowess as possible.

Boil your concept down to its quintessence, so if you must describe your project quickly to harried and impatient agents, producers, money or programming people, you will be able to get the whole thing across fast and with conviction. This is always impressive and puts you ahead of the pack.

These are experiential tips that you can promptly absorb. They are not specific instructions but are my way of guiding you through the first stages of creating and pitching your material. You will achieve nothing if there isn't a bright, initial spark. Add to this the real desire to persevere until something happens. Before we explore any marketing or psychological specifics, I want to stress that enthusiasm and consistency of approach are elemental to getting your work on the air. Unless the quality of your product is downright rank, you will achieve positive results of some kind if you take care of these basics.

Chapter Three:
Do You Really Want to Do This?

YOU HAVE WRITTEN A MASTERFUL TV MOVIE ABOUT A HOUSE-wife who decides to become a stage actress against the advice of her friends and children but persists and ends up on Broadway. You have based it on someone you know, you have some knowledge of the theater, and you just love your script. But suddenly, from a place of exultation and personal satisfaction you pass into a place of recurrent rejections and stonewalling on the part of agents, producers, whomever. The script doesn't sell, and some of these brokers have the criminal audacity to say that your script is not good enough, or too good, or not right at this time, or not right for this company. A feeling of intense failure comes over you and you don't know what to do about it.

If you are thin-skinned and can't take much criticism or rejection, this is not the business for you. Of course, you may feel that even if you are unsuited, you are so determined to make this your career that you will learn to live with the annoyance. If that is the case, you won't be discouraged by the truth about the general state of acceptance of writing for TV.

If you are thoroughly determined to be a television writer and have built-in patience and endurance, you will toss your hair back, turn the word processor on, and get to it again, severely revising your script — maybe it should be about a divorced house-wife who wants to become a social worker. With a minimum of fuss and self-pity, you are back on the road to a positive outcome: either a success (a sale) that results from your progress along the learning curve or at least a more informed picture of what "they" want. If this kind of process is inconceivable to you, then write as a hobby and see what happens, but don't allow it to become your "day job" because it will involve too much unnecessary pain.

Some people fit right into the commercial TV world. A canny sense of what will be accepted seems to be almost innate with some writers. Most of us, however, must run the gauntlet of rejection before we start breaking through. You may find it hard to imagine your kind of writing appearing on "NBC Movie of the Week" or prime-time network sitcoms. You may grow into these genres, or perhaps you should be aiming at public television or pay cable TV. Then again, perhaps you should be concentrating on writing for documentaries.

What are the odds against your work being accepted by the television establishment? What forms of duress must almost every writer endure before he achieves success? It is useful to consider this first of all. If you are not really committed, you will know early on that this is not the vocation for you. If you like quick results and are congenitally impatient, this is not the business for you. If you're patient and thick-skinned, on the other hand, you won't be vacillating constantly between joy and despair and puzzlement.

These are the only emotional warnings needed. Most of you who are full of enthusiasm about writing will not be discouraged by any of that; after all, any job worth having entails a great deal of sacrifice and disappointment. Persistence will override all the stops and starts. Sooner or later you will learn what it is inside you that is capable of being transformed into a television production.

Maintaining Your Energy

It doesn't hurt to think about some of the keys to maintaining your energy as a writer even before you get seriously into the business. Positive thinking, as in any other area of living, is essential to success in writing. When no boss or supervisor is telling you that you are on the right path or that your writing is great or needs work or whatever, your morale can become severely taxed. Pitching is even more difficult, as it is hard to get good advice except from the very people you are pitching to. If you are in the early phases of looking for an agent or even if you are actively pitching your writing to producers, you must stay on top of your submissions while keeping up your confidence, energy level and enthusiasm.

You should never rely on just one pathway or entrée. Keep your options open at all times, and have several fires burning simultaneously so that you increase the odds of acceptance. This requires some subtlety, because in the actual process of submitting scripts — as any agent worth her salt will tell you — you can't be selling your wares all over town, particularly if you are dealing with the Hollywood establishment. Executives or producers getting wind that a particular script is also in the hands of a myriad of their competitors can work against you. However, just to complicate life, sometimes it is important to be pursuing multiple, simultaneous paths to the same goal. You just have to suss out the situation and be as discreet as you can. Also, working on several things at the same time can sometimes be a good way to achieve success. You may have a concept, a one-liner, a treatment, a script — all different projects — all possible to pitch here and there at the same time. Again, don't go berserk with this and spread yourself too thin, but it can be better for you psychologically if all your eggs are not in one basket; this can help mitigate your disappointment if there is little or no success with a single project.

"Good" and "Bad" Producers

The television industry has as many good people running it as any other intensely commercial sector of modern society. It also has a substantial proportion of schmucks, sharks and snakes, out for themselves and with little regard for other people's feelings or original ideas. There is no rule about how to discriminate between the good and bad elements. Trust your instincts.

It is better in the long run to deal with people who are known in the industry and have at least produced or been involved in some way with legitimate broadcasting. Logically, you might argue, "Well, yes, but *I'm* unknown and can hardly be called legitimate based on my track record, so why should I adopt this attitude?" It's a good question; nevertheless, it is better for you as a beginner to meet with and work with professionals who are widely trusted if not liked.

People in the television business are usually overworked and pressured. While you may not take an immediate liking to the prospective agent, story editor or producer, you must trust who you are dealing with. Whenever I have gone against my basic instincts on this, I have taken some kind of fall.

For example, I was recently asked to meet a "producer" who had optioned a novel and wanted someone to write the screenplay. I met with him and was immediately turned off by his attitude. He was evasive, he didn't know when the film would be produced, he didn't seem on top of things. Yet his office was impressive, and he had at least six people working for him, also in nice offices. The meeting was on a Friday and he asked me to read the novel, nearly a thousand pages long, over the weekend. It was a real job on that hot summer weekend, but I read it and made copious notes in the margins. Monday came and he was nowhere to be found. He had probably left the city to escape the heat and just hadn't come back. Some days later, I managed to get him on the phone. Without even apologizing for making me do a rush job unnecessarily, he mumbled something about having found another writer and not needing me.

I was disgusted—the novel wasn't even enjoyable—but I put the phone down and vowed to trust my better judgments forever after. Maybe I was a little foolish to embark on an unpaid reading job, but sometimes it's okay to do that. I didn't feel 100 percent about the project, yet I did the reading anyway. Never again. I hadn't trusted him from the moment I saw him nervously fingering his beard. Suffice to say that your stomach often has the real answer to your questions about the caliber of the folks you encounter in the business.

Later in this book are interviews with executives and the like from these different fields. These will give you a better idea of what your chances are in any given area. There are enough honest, hard-working people in television to ease the burden of entry. The warnings I issued earlier are to alert you to the possibility of encountering carpetbaggers and hustlers.

The "Piece of Paper"

If you are keen to write for nonfiction genres, the situation is different. Much of this kind of programming comes from independent sources with little or no money. If you are assigned to work under these circumstances, or if you write something and someone wants to produce it but cannot pay you immediately, try to get that proverbial "piece of paper." Even a short letter of agreement is better than nothing and will hold up in court if there is some chicanery. The crucial thing is feeling comfortable about doing the work. If you are nursing a grudge about your talent being abused in some way, it will usually be reflected in your work. So be rigorous in checking your feelings about your place in the production. Deferred payment is commonplace in the world of documentaries, but you should be offered some assurances.

In the 1980s many books were published, lectures given, and support groups assembled to help people verify their self-worth in some way. One of the constants among these therapies is the need to sensitize the individual to his actual financial worth. Falling into a pattern of working for nothing is psychologically unhealthy, unless you are wealthy and want it that way. To become a successful professional you should be paid a fair wage. Too often, beginners are enticed into "freebies." There is nothing wrong with being an intern, the modern equivalent of the Renaissance apprentice, but there comes a time when enough is enough. Being exploited is a common complaint of the writer and other artists. Simply draw the line when it feels right to do that. If a producer persists in not paying you or in evading your entreaties for money, stop working for that person. I feel quite passionately about this, having made too many mistakes in this area in my younger, greener years. Once you have proven that you have what it takes, go for the money and enjoy the sense of achievement from supporting yourself through your craft.

Avoiding Formula

Being a mass media artist is a relatively new occupation. It demands a new combo/formula of skills: creative talent, writing power, strong media perceptions and observations, and astute marketing ability. Being a mass media artist for the nineties and beyond demands a thorough, current knowledge of where TV is going and what its forever-expanding parameters imply about your own twist on the writing profession. What should I write next? Should it be something I've always wanted to write or should it be topical, even trendy, so that I will garner quick and real interest from the producers and programmers? Is that kind of strategically surgical approach to marketing my writing a healthy thing for my work or not?

Sometimes when you are watching a television program of some sort you feel instinctively that it was created and produced to an exact formula—like a fast-food item—strictly to make money and grab an audience without regard to substance or lasting value. This is not an achievement worth spending half your life on, unless of course your only interest is money and accumulating wealth. Some writers *are* only interested in making lots of money, and good luck to them, but I intuit that most creative artists, even those working in the undeniably crass world of broadcast television, want more than financial success. They write because they have something to say and it almost hurts if they can't get it out on paper and then on the screen.

TV Writing as a Career

The best reason to go into TV writing is twofold: First, you are a creative artist, either fascinated by fictional or nonfictional works; second, you would like to take a chance on making your living with your creative abilities, and TV writing is a completely modern, commercial field, where, if you succeed, you can forget about having to work at a job you don't like. This commixture of imagination and a prophesying yet pragmatic mind is special and isn't at all easy to pull off. You face powerful and always formidable competition in the television field. There are only so many hours of programming to fill and then there's a vacuum wherein float thousands of unproduced screenplays, treatments and proposals.

Yet, if you want to break away from nine-to-five tedium and take a shot at the communication game, aspiring to succeed as a TV creator is actually very sensible. Your work will probably prove to be much harder than any nine-to-five gig, but it can afford you enormous satisfaction and rewards, financial and otherwise. So the very source of wanting to write for television must be this carefully considered thought based on an uncarefully felt emotional state. You feel the impulse to write and feel it strongly enough to want to actually base your life on it—you know, food, shelter, children, and so on. If you can truthfully say that you are not at all put off by the obvious difficulties and convolutions involved in becoming and staying a professional writer, you should get moving as soon as possible.

It is also possible to write part-time. The problem with this approach is also twofold. In the stage where you are trying to break into the industry, you will almost certainly be compelled to do other jobs in order to keep body and soul together. So when you finally achieve the exalted status of supporting yourself by your writing, you won't want to divide your time up. You will need all your days and many of your nights to continue to write for a living.

Added to this is the commitment factor. Until you decide absolutely that this is what you want to do and until you take action to prove this, both to yourself and anyone else you have to deal with, you have not really taken the leap. Now, shading professionally into producer or director or editor is fine. Wherever your own genuine momentum takes you is where you want to be and, most likely, should be. The passion and dedication necessary to achieve fulfillment as a TV writer can usually be generated regularly only by someone who goes at it day in, day out.

The key to success in TV writing (or in any of the mass media) is your conviction that this is the vocation for you. Even if you can't truthfully say that, then you can resolve to give it your best shot. A driving determination both to write consistently and not to be discouraged but to press on with the work you believe in is necessary to have the guts to deal with what is going to be thrown at you.

Chapter Four:

FICTION: WRITING TO GET IT SOLD

THE DREAM IS TO SELL A SCREENPLAY TO TELEVISION AND BE propelled on the road to a lifelong career in creating dramas for massive audiences. People do it, hundreds of them—why not you? The dream can be turned into reality.

Before You Start

Before we get down to it, however, ask yourself these four questions:

1. Am I talented?
2. Which genre do I like; what am I genuinely suited for?
3. Do I have a great idea?
4. Do I have the sense of strategy and the knowledge of how to get to the necessary conduits for me to sell this thing?

When you have satisfied yourself that you are now firm in your convictions, read on. This is not a scriptwriting book, so I won't go into detail about the writing craft, except as it relates to clear salability. What are the basics?

Getting an Agent

Script readers, agents and producers are overworked. They may seem to be far-off figures, inhabiting the glamorous world of show business, but they spend much of their time in the essential mode of looking for new material. None of them can grow and prosper without constantly watching for new fictional work. So they read and study incoming work by both neophyte and known writers, who are, then, all in competition with each other, even if they never see each other's work or actually meet. Do your best not to start out behind the pack. Not knowing the way to present your work is the silliest way to put yourself out of the running.

Let's start by hypothesizing that you are trying to get an agent—the most pragmatic way to enter the business. How do you go about this?

First, contact the Writers' Guild, either the East or West branch, and get their list of reputable agents. Write to: The Writers' Guild West, 8955 Beverly Boulevard, West Hollywood, CA 90048, (213) 550-1000; or The Writers' Guild East, 555 West 57th Street, New York, NY 10019, (212) 245-6180. You do not have to be a member of the Guild to ask for this information. Each agency, large or small, has a client list that you can send for to find out which would be the most appropriate for you. You may have to do some research first, just to discover which writers are doing the kind of television you are aiming at. If you are only interested in episodic television writing, for instance, you should watch a few of those shows and make a note of the writers and producers, who are not always household names.

This shouldn't be such a chore because you should be studying these shows in any case to become au fait with what they are like and their basic forms.

Identify likely agents and decide which one(s) you think might be interested. Simply check their addresses. Then phone them and get enough information to actually write them a letter. Next, write your chosen agent or agents a query letter.

The Query Letter

Let the agents know what you have to offer by condensing your script idea into a sentence or two, and ask them whether this is appropriate for their agency. The key to this is your ability to be succinct about your idea and to give them the impression that you are both focused and somewhat humble. Try not to suggest that your idea is the greatest thing since *Gone with the Wind*, because this will put them off. However, you should express confidence, professionalism and enthusiasm.

Already we are walking several fine lines, but this is something you should quickly get used to. And even though this isn't the easiest task, it is a challenge to your communication skills. You are, after all, professing talent as a writer. If the very first piece of writing they ever see from you gets your idea and talent across, however minimally, you are making good progress. If, conversely, your letter is awkward, you are loading the dice unnecessarily against yourself.

Let's suppose you have written a script for a weekly one-hour episodic show called "Donna West, D.E.A.," a show about a glamorous, blond, female undercover D.E.A. agent whose specialty is busting major league drug dealers. She has a male partner, Harry Mercer, and works out of New York City and Miami. She is often in several kinds of jeopardy (something the networks usually demand for crime shows, especially those involving female protagonists). The show is in its third season and has achieved the usual amount of publicity. People know it, and it seems set for several more seasons of top-twenty Nielsen success. Here are two possible query letters, the first lousy, the second good.

A Bad Letter

Dear Mr. Weinberger:
I am writing to you because I have written a truly great episode of "Donna West, D.E.A." I am certain that it would be a big hit, and if you ask me, the series could use a new slant. In my episode, Donna will fall in love with the notorious coke dealer, José Fernandez, who also happens to be a double murderer. She leaves her job to join him in Colombia, where they lead an extravagant lifestyle for a year or two. He keeps drugging her with this new psycho-drug called Schizo-2. Donna is, however, genuinely fond of him and continues to love him after the drug wears off. She becomes a basket weaver and socialite. There are five Uzi gun battles in the show and eleven car chases, culminating in a chase

across two South American countries between a D.E.A. Rolls Royce and a customized F-16 owned by Fernandez. We see the spectacular destruction of three jets and fifteen expensive cars. I have created a new permanent character for the show called Leftie Banks, a black, gay undercover cop who frequently has liaisons with gay amyl nitrate dealers. I know this will grab both the gay and the druggie demographic. I feel your agency will benefit from my joining the roster. I would like to meet with you sometime in the next few days, before I go to Hawaii for my vacation.

Can't wait,

Jim

If you talk with agents, they will probably tell you that they get letters almost this far off the mark. Let's analyze the problems with the letter.

First, never say that what you have written is "truly great" or "terrific" or anything remotely like that. Self-congratulation is the certain sign of a beginner and of a self-deceiving one at that. It is simply not for you to judge the quality of your writing. Any experienced agent will immediately be turned off by that kind of false confidence, seeing it as a sign of gross inexperience and insecurity.

To suggest that what you have created is a "certain hit" is dangerous and presumptuous and will alienate the agent immediately. Avoid phrases like "if you ask me" — nobody asked you, and in any case, it is far too familiar. "The series could use a new slant" is not something to say, for several reasons. You could not know that, and your comment is negative. It is patronizing and certain death for your image.

Now we get to the outline. The letter writer is correct in including an outline, but this one, besides being indicative of a completely awful series of ideas, is far too long. I can see the agent's eyes glazing over.

While we're at it, let's look at the actual story line suggested and see what is wrong. Protagonists of crime shows rarely make the kind of mistake that Donna is supposedly making here. If she did, she would never be allowed to go on making it for two years.

The descriptions of the pursuit sequences are too detailed; the sequences themselves are quite impossible, given the relatively modest budgets of episodic television. This one would be more appropriate for a forty-million-dollar James Bond feature movie.

The introduction of a new "permanent character" is an absolute mistake. It is hard enough to push yourself onto the staff of an existing show, let alone come in with a new character. As it is, the new character created here is far too off-the-wall to be taken seriously. As outlandish as network television can be sometimes, it is still basically conservative. Leftie Banks would never make it to the TV screen.

The sentence "I know this will grab both the gay and the druggie demographic" is also completely unacceptable. First, you could never "know" this. Second, steer clear of any pretentious statements like this in a query letter. Demographics are not your concern yet, if ever.

At all costs avoid making arrogant statements like "I feel your agency will benefit from my joining the roster." The last sentence is the most unacceptable item in the whole letter. Never tell a busy agent, or producer for that matter, when he or she should meet you. You must show humility in this and meet when it is convenient for *them*, even if it takes weeks or months. And don't end with familiarities such as "Can't wait" or "Jim" — they suggest a closeness that, of course, does not yet exist.

Now, this letter is worse than most, but the hyperbole of badness is there so that you can see the worst case and learn from it.

A Good Letter

Dear Mr. Weinberger:

I am a writer and am interested in your representing me. I understand you represent Barry Fine and Anne Kershaw, and I thought that you might be attracted to my work, which is in the same genre.

Specifically, I want to write a show for the ABC series "Donna West, D.E.A." and have, I believe, a valid script for presentation to the show's producers.

My show involves Donna posing undercover as a glamorous

businesswoman who supposedly wants to gain favor with powerful clients by throwing seductively wild parties where cocaine
and champagne are on every table. She lures a top South American drug dealer into a deal, intending to consummate a sting
against his cartel. The twist is that he falls in love with her, even
after discovering her true identity. This is a new variation for the
show that could add a new dimension to her character both as a
woman and as a professional.

I wrote extensively for my student newspaper and wish to pursue a career in television. I would appreciate your considering me
as a client. Thanking you in anticipation,

Yours sincerely,

James Blanding

This letter may seem too self-effacing, but there is no reason
at this point to act in any other way. The idea will speak for itself,
at least in terms of getting you an appointment with the agent.
The likelihood is that, if he or she wants to give you a chance,
there will be a reply asking you to send an example of your writing. The agent might ask for a treatment, but these days the agent
will probably ask you for an actual script. This does mean a lot
of work for you without remuneration, but at the beginning of
a writing career there is no other way to go. Agents are tough
customers — they have to be — but they are always looking for new
talent, and there is no reason why they should not want to look
at your work, if the query letter is acceptable.

If the first one you write to rejects the idea of even looking at
your work, then calmly accept that and move on to another agent
or agency. It may take several tries, but if there is anything there
at all in your letter, someone will accept the bait fairly soon, and
you are on your way.

Do not write to an agent unless you have a substantial piece of
work ready to be sent. It would be a mistake to get someone
interested and then have to put something together quickly to
show your worth. Desperate hurrying never makes for quality
work, unless you are exceptional.

Conform to the Formatting Tradition

Formatting a script properly is very important. Sending something, however brilliant, that doesn't conform at least roughly to the accepted layout will alienate agents, script readers and producers. In the trance of creative excitement, people sometimes forget to do the silliest things, like putting their name, address and telephone number on a front page attached to the script. You should have already registered your work with the Writers' Guild; say so on this front page. Put the title of the work in the middle of the page. If it is to be submitted as an episode for an episodic or sitcom series already on the air, make that clear. There is no hard-and-fast rule for how to do this, so simply be clear about it. Say something like " 'Dangerous Love' – an episode for 'Donna West, D.E.A.' " Put your name, address and phone number toward the bottom right of the page, and the reference to the Writers' Guild registration at the bottom left. Specify whether you registered at the East or West branch of the Guild.

Successful Scriptwriting by Jurgen Wolff and Kerry Cox, published by Writer's Digest Books, is a very helpful guide to the details of formatting scripts for television, as well as giving thoroughly helpful pointers about content and style. The authors suggest a sixty-page script for episodic TV (a page corresponds roughly to one minute of air time); it should be in four acts. A movie-of-the-week, which takes up two hours on television, is actually about ninety-four minutes, given the standard number of commercials included within it, so the teleplay length should be between ninety and one hundred pages, depending on how much dialogue and how much action there is in the script. A situation comedy would be about twenty-four pages.

A Successful Hollywood Writer

Lee Aronsohn is a very successful mainstream Hollywood writer. He made his mark on the massively popular "The Love Boat" series, a huge network hit in the United States that is still playing in reruns here and literally all over the world. In the story of his rise to success, we can see the way one man did it.

Lee was a stand-up comedian, working places like The Comedy Store in Los Angeles. He wanted to write for network TV, however, and at one point simply put together a list of everybody he knew who might know someone who might know someone, and so on. As he put it, he had "lunch with everybody." A writer from "The Love Boat" had seen him perform and asked him whether he had considered writing for television. In the first season of the series, Aronsohn wrote a spec script for the show. He obtained sample scripts of the program and did his best to imitate them in his own way.

As Lee says, it is a mistake to try and improve upon the series you want to write for—just try to copy it as best you can. It took him almost a year to actually get on the show's team of writers, but he succeeded. And he says it wasn't that difficult; he just persevered and concentrated on his goal. Aronsohn also debunks the myth that there are masses of talented yet unemployed writers "out there." "If you are competent, you will work," he says. "You need to write a reasonably funny script in the proper form and capture the rhythms of the series." According to him, producers are usually desperate to find people who have this facility.

Lee wrote twenty-one episodes of "The Love Boat," sometimes writing one of the three stories per show, sometimes two. From this series he went on to other shows, including the ratings success "Charles in Charge," for which he wrote thirteen shows over three years. He did an episode of "Who's the Boss?" and then Columbia hired him away. Next he did five episodes of "Everything's Relative" and then went back to "Charles in Charge." What we see in Aronsohn is a highly pragmatic, talented professional able to get work fairly easily once he proved that he could master the basic form.

Lee proudly calls himself a journeyman writer. He suggests that anyone who wants to emulate his career should definitely watch the shows. He recommends writing two spec scripts for two different types of shows. After all is said and done, he feels that TV scriptwriting is a craft more than an art, catering to a young audience with a short attention span. Aronsohn also advises that, in order to make it as a comedy writer, you must live in Los Angeles.

Lee actually had no agent at all for three years or so, progressing on the basis of personal relationships. Although he admits that most writers end up using an agent, he personally doesn't see it as the best way to get ahead. Just keep trying, he says, and meeting people and pestering them until they see that you can do the work and can be relied on to keep pumping it out.

What you can learn from this writer, who now has a very lucrative job developing concepts for Lorimar, is that it's up to you. If you set your sights realistically and then go for it, without letting anyone put you off track, eventually you will break through. TV always needs too much product to ignore people who are truly unrelenting in their efforts to get into the TV writers' inner circle.

Common Sense

Common sense should be your motto where pitching is concerned. Unless you feel that you are in a unique situation — where you've secured some kind of seminepotistic connection or have written a very unusual piece that just doesn't fit into normal categories — then you should conform to what is expected. This doesn't make you remiss or formulaic — it just gets you in the door in the right way and stops prospective buyers from being put off right from the get go. Remember, the originality and fire of creativity lies in the writing itself, not in the presentation. Let the work speak for itself — don't feel the need to hype it or yourself. To be conventional in this stage of the game is to be smart, and therefore potentially successful.

Chapter Five:

FICTION GENRES

IN ORDER TO GIVE YOURSELF THE GREATEST POSSIBLE CHANCE for success, it is imperative that you go for the genre that best fits your inner contours and outer aims. This involves not only looking at what is the natural creative path for you to follow, but also projecting the kind of pitching and selling that your chosen genre will require.

There are exceptions to the categories discussed here, but the lists cover 95 percent of what gets produced. Let's go through them and I will briefly explain the ramifications of opting for one or the other.

Episodics

In the 1980s, this form expanded from previous times, with crime shows still making up the majority of network fare. Shows such as "Hunter," "Magnum, P.I.," "Spenser: for Hire," and "Miami Vice" continued to be very popular, continuing the tradition started by "Highway Patrol," "Dragnet," and later, "Kojak" and "Columbo." Crime shows are a little more sophisticated these days, employing more humor and more psychological depth. They also tend to be more violent, reflecting the increase of violent crime in the seventies, eighties and nineties in the major metropolitan areas.

Actors like Robert Urich, Don Johnson and Philip Michael Thomas brought a new panache to their roles, both in the way they behaved and in their styles. "Miami Vice" added fashion and rock music components to the episodic recipe. "Midnight Caller" moved the focus of suspense from law enforcement to the media. "Quantum Leap" and "Alien Nation" brought fantasy and science fiction to the medium. The basic formula remained, however. Variations on murder, robbery, kidnapping and drug dealing were still the staples. As baby boomers became the major consumers in the marketplace, these shows were increasingly aimed at viewers between the ages of eighteen and thirty-five.

This bulge in the demographics also brought success to series like "Hill Street Blues" and "L.A. Law," which took a more complex approach to crime fighting and social problems such as abortion and drug abuse. "Tour of Duty" and "China Beach" echoed the socially realistic approach to war drama successfully produced in feature movies like *Platoon*. Even the successful "thirtysomething," a mixture of light drama and social realism, attempts to address serious issues, though they are clouded by the flippant strains of yuppie woe. More traditional fare like "McGyver" and "The Father Dowling Mysteries" continues to be produced relentlessly. Horror episodics such as "Tales from the Dark Side," "Friday the Thirteenth," and "She-Wolf of London" have become very popular in the early nineties. A series like "Midnight Caller" shows much more maturity, probing relationships and social problems. Most of this points to a more humane trend in episodic television, though it must be added that the main recipe still favors guns, violence, whodunits, and general criminal mayhem. Shows like "Cagney and Lacey" mix crime and social issues quite well, showing more multidimensional characters, giving scriptwriters more to play with, and allowing a better use of language. I sense that the trend is toward more mature programming—the buying power is still in the hands of that part of the population now in their thirties and forties, people nurtured intellectually in the socially conscious sixties.

Though serious subject matter is still more the province of two-hour, made-for-TV movies, it seems that even the crime-and-chase episodics are a little deeper in content than they were. This makes it more of a writers' medium than ever, as action is a touch less prevalent in the weekly series and dialogue that much more important. Even back in the days of "The Rockford Files," James Garner's lines were witty and compassionate, rather than macho and tough sounding.

"Hill Street Blues" and "L.A. Law," both put out by the innovative Steven Bochco, set a new standard of writing, with their episodes-within-episodes style, jumping from one lead character and situation to another, more like the modern novel than traditional TV. One can only hope that the public will continue to support shows of the quality of "St. Elsewhere" and "Moonlighting," both gone now but still influential. It is interesting to note that in the 1990 Fall season, the already innovative Bochco went out on a limb with his series "Cop Rock" for ABC Network, a serious cop show where songs break out in the middle of the action like in an old-time musical. On the surface, it may not seem like a great idea, but Bochco had struck gold before where angels feared to tread. (Not this time, however; the show was cancelled.)

More recently, the genre was expanded by the sensational rage/ cult classic "Twin Peaks." This essentially auteur series by David Lynch, as weird as it is, should be an encouragement for new writers. Younger audiences demand that programmers reach out into new forms and dramatic areas. Dreams, fantasies and inner states are going to be more a part of TV drama than ever before.

The other subgenre in episodic television encompasses the "Dynasty," "Dallas," "Falcon Crest" shows, where the glamour and sin of the high life is examined in soapy detail week after week. These shows are rarely open to new writers, as they demand strict adherence to formula plots and only very occasionally go off the beaten thematic path of high finance, adultery, corporate betrayal and the like. Again, writing a sample show might get you in the door by showing an agent or producer that you do have the kind of specialized talent necessary to manufacture this kind of writing. Then it is a question of who he or she knows and whether there are any gaps in the writing teams, all based in Hollywood. These scripts are not particularly difficult to write as the standards are, frankly, very low, so it might be easier to make one of these shows your first try at the business. Although "Dallas" and "Dynasty" seem to have reached the end of their long runs, new ones will undoubtedly spring up—unless the general public shows a surprising new collective discrimination which finally says no to this kind of pulp video.

Study the Shows

If you want to write for one of these shows, you must study the show. See as many episodes as you can and take careful note of the trends within the series. Also, it is not a bad idea to actually write an episode based on what you know from simply watching the program, just so that you can show an agent or someone at the production company that you have the basic writing talent and discipline to stay in the groove of a specific series. A sample script, written in a professional manner, is a good thing to have. It can prove to the agent or story editor that you can write consistently in the style of the show. Even if the agent or other creative/industry broker does not feel that he can immediately present it to the production company, if he likes the work it will represent your talent and will put you in his files. If a project comes up, you have already made your impression.

Sample Script

Episodics are always made by established production companies or "suppliers" who in turn have their established writers. If you want to write this kind of television, you have to watch the shows, write a complete script, and then find an agent who already has a relationship with the production company. If your script is very, very good, it stands a chance of getting you in the door. Some suppliers, however, do not look outside their stable of writers for new blood because of the high cost of production and the need for writers who understand budget as well as story line and characterization.

This kind of work often comes after some paying of dues, writing on spec, and exploiting any contacts you can find. Companies have story line intensives before the production season starts, where they map out changes and movements within scripting, and only the established team of writers is privy to these inner circle subtleties. How are you to know what the producers' plans are for the upcoming season unless you are at these inside conferences? Nevertheless, if you write something with great merit, it will be considered.

Sitcoms

Situation comedy is the staple of network and syndicated rerun TV. Newer "alternative" networks like Fox and pay-per-view cable TV's Home Box Office and Showtime also produce sitcoms, so the field is an ever-widening one and one that is not likely to go away in the foreseeable future. The genre started with the classic "I Love Lucy," Burns and Allen, and Phil Silvers shows of the fifties that had evolved out of radio comedies of the previous decade. By the late eighties, sitcoms had become multifaceted. They are now done on both videotape and film; they range from extremely light, family-oriented shows to somewhat sophisticated series like "Fresh Prince of Bel Air," which at the time it premiered was up-to-the-second and hip and broke a lot of the rules. Nevertheless, the basic premise remains the same: a group of characters dealing with different challenging situations creating laughs. Exaggeration is the name of the game, the lead characters often being simply comedy cartoon figures. Shows like "Cosby" have made the form more realistic, basing their humor on funny domestic moments and even serious encounters. The sitcom is not, however, supposed to be serious in the main, and an aspiring writer in this genre should aim for rapid-fire comedic action.

To get into the world of situation comedy, write a full script before you send the query letter to an agent. It is also not out of the question to send your work straight to the production company, but I believe this diminishes your chances of getting it accepted. Nevertheless, if you have a singular feel for this kind of writing, there is no reason why you shouldn't try. If the person who receives your work sees a gleam of talent in the words, it can't do you any harm, even if you don't get hired immediately because of it.

Inventing a whole new sitcom may not be the most practical way to get work, but it will certainly show an agent how innovative and funny you can be. And you never know; sometimes, a show business pro will see something new that she thinks will stimulate the interest of one of her connections. Then you are set off down the road of finding a known producer or production company to attach yourself to. New writers *have* created new shows.

The main thing to remember succeeding in the sitcom field is that you must develop a good sense of what will make the public laugh and you must be very persistent. In the seventies, when I was producing with the Television Laboratory at Channel 13, WNET-TV, in New York City, we employed an administrative assistant named Diane English. She was exceptional at her job; she was also a lot of fun to be around and very humorous.

Seventeen years later her name is all over the big hit CBS sitcom series, "Murphy Brown," starring Candice Bergen. English created this show, and she and her husband, Joel Shukovsky, are the executive producers. She is considered a real heavy in mainstream American television. It was obvious even back then that she would do good work, but now that I think about it, it makes a great deal of sense that she should have emerged so ultra-successful in network television. She was totally determined and very inventive. Eventually she broke through in a big way. Her success should be encouraging to anyone who wants to get into TV comedy.

Writing for sitcoms as a newcomer is a good idea if you have a genuine feel for the form. Some people are very funny at dinner parties but are not funny on paper. Others are good gagsters but have no feeling for plot and characterization. You have to have all these things going for you. If you do, and you feel strongly about doing this for a living, there are several points I must make.

Four Basic Pointers

1. Decide whether you want to write for an existing show. If you do, you must remember that, just as is the case in episodic

television, inside writers hold the secrets and you do not. Plans are made for sitcom characters in advance.

2. If you do not want to write for a show already on the air, then you are talking about creating a whole new idea and pitching this to a production company. This puts you in the position of a quasi producer, having to create interest in a concept. You will most likely have to attach yourself to a known producer or writer to get your idea noticed.

3. You should know that this is a potentially dangerous situation (and not comic by any means) you are putting yourself in, because comedy concepts can be stolen, adapted and resubmitted by another person. Registering at the Writers' Guild (East or West) is crucial. In order to achieve some success, it is better to work with someone else experienced in the business and proceed as a team with some leverage. If you have direct contacts with sitcom people, then feel free to use them—if you trust them.

4. To become a sitcom writing professional, it is almost mandatory that you move to Los Angeles. These series are intense collaborations, and you have to be there, on the job, not on the other end of a telephone, to function as a writer. All of the sitcoms come out of Los Angeles, so this is an inescapable requirement for success if this is the way you want to go. Sure, your original pitching can be done from your own town, but if something clicks and the people with the power want your show produced or want you to join an existent team, then you have to go west. Not that this is any burden, once you get cooking. Los Angeles may have pollution and traffic jams, but it also has a perfectly congenial atmosphere for writing comedy. A successful life in this kind of TV writing will be a lot of fun as well as lucrative.

Movies-of-the-Week

Television in the United States has evolved to a place that was the exclusive domain of British television up to a few years ago. Now, TV movies are often about social issues and give a writer the opportunity to do quality work and not to be turned down out of hand.

This, then, would seem to be the place for the creative writer. No formulas, no subjects that are strictly verboten, plenty of range. The made-for-TV movie is probably one of the best ways to break into writing fiction for television.

I do not advise looking at the current crop of made-for-TV movies and choosing one of those categories so as to be fashionable or gain acceptance. It is better to forget the content of the myriad TV movies already produced and simply go with your instincts about what you want to write about. The development of your idea from its germination to getting it on the screen, while not as lengthy a process as making a feature movie, will still take an average of two years. Trying to capitalize on a trend that has already manifested in a TV movie or two means, in any case, that you are borrowing from something several years old. Better to watch the movies-of-the-week just to observe the tone and level of quality involved, plus the repeatable structure—how many acts, where the commercials fall, the ratio of action to dialogue, the overall topicality, the kind of actors usually employed, recurrent directors, and so on.

TV movies break down into seven acts, allowing for commercial breaks. At an unseen level, the deeper psychological and dramatic structure still has three acts like a theatrical movie script. During the writing of the script it is worth making sure that at the end of each of the seven acts you create some suspense, not necessarily involving violence or jeopardy, but enough given the context of the story to keep the viewer interested and eager to see the next part of the film.

Finding Subjects

Here are some ways of finding subject matter: First and foremost, if there is something that positively grips you and you feel that it will not be rejected out of hand by a network, then go with it until someone tells you that it is out of the question. Even then, persist if you really believe in it with your head and your heart.

These days, networks seem to like subjects that are of general interest, the kind of stories dealt with on local news programs and covered in *Newsweek*, *Time* and *People*. All the better if one of these issues has personal significance for you—a story told from direct experience always stands a good chance of having those nuances and details that make a film believable and compelling. On the other hand, seeing something in the newspaper that grabs you should prompt you to do further research, maybe even leading you to the story's source and acquiring the rights to it. This can sometimes mean money changing hands and sometimes not, depending on the people involved.

Say, for instance, you see something about a newsworthy event that has obvious human drama, like a natural disaster or a plane crash. Making sure that you stay within the bounds of discretion and avoid ambulance chasing or impinging on the privacy of the individuals involved, seek out the main "protagonists" and inquire whether the story has been acquired by anybody else. If not, there is no reason why you shouldn't get a hold on it first and proceed to extrapolate from the bare facts a story line that does not offend the individuals involved.

Obviously, a story that you can actually get all the facts about is preferable to something involving the military or state secrets or the like. If it is an extensively covered story, seasoned professionals in the field will most likely have already made their entrée, though this is not always the case. It's a little like avoiding the rush hour traffic only to find to your dismay that everybody else had the same idea. The roads may actually be quiet at rush hour. Take a shot.

One of the most important slants to consider in choosing a subject to present to a producing entity or broker is whether the main characters in your movie have universal appeal. They must show the ability to change—or if they are static, that at least must be the point of the tale told. The audience as a whole must be able to identify with them. Networks will never be keen on simply showing geniuses at work or big business moguls reaping the benefits of their wealth and power—the latter has now become the plot jurisdiction of the prime time high budget soaps like "Dynasty." A success coming from humble beginnings is of strong interest; a triumph over adversity is usually thought of as having mass interest. Sportsmen with handicaps, children with severe diseases, performers with drinking or drug problems, housewives with strong ambition, "little people" fighting the system in some way—these are the types of character situations that have strong, broad appeal.

The idea is to move the audience in whatever way you can. Pitching and selling a script that is in any way abstract or purely discoursive or intellectual is virtually impossible—at least to the major networks and HBO. PBS's "American Playhouse" has a much more broad-minded attitude, but even there, you have to honor the age-old unwritten rules of drama—that it should be based on conflict, development and resolution.

Should You Write a Whole Script?

If you are a beginning writer, it is better to complete the whole script before presenting it to anybody. If you do finish it, make sure you register it. If you emerge with just the concept, an outline, or even a treatment, the idea can be turned down and then stolen. And there's very little you can do about it, even if you acquired the rights. An unscrupulous producer can always take the idea, find another angle, and then weasel his way into reacquiring the rights using the temptations of big money and a powerful organization. If a script is completed, this is much harder to do.

As a beginner, you must prove your ability to write a full script. Even if it isn't wonderfully executed, if a producer or agent sees the essence of a good film, he will either prompt you to improve it with the benefit of his feedback or, at worst, buy it from you and assign it to a known writer. If this happens, incidentally, it may not be a bad way for you to break into the business, even though it might seem very unfair at the outset.

Writing the script is most likely only going to prove to the prospective buyer that you can write. It is unlikely that a network will buy a completed script from you, mainly because they almost always want strong input into a script they are going to produce for one or two million dollars. The usual pattern is for a production company or an agent to show a positive response to your script, then ask you if you have any concepts for other movies-of-the-week. I am aware that this seems a trifle ridiculous, but it is the tradition in a business that can't afford to spend millions on unknown writers and won't, unless the teleplay is outstanding.

The initial writing sample, which could be a completed script, will most likely serve as a calling card. But if it is liked, it is well worth the months of effort you put into it, because it opens the door. Then, if you have other good ideas, a bright production company will escort you to the network programmers and lead you through the labyrinth of TV acceptance.

Persistence and humility are bottom-line necessities at this stage. Pitching in this context is more a matter of showing your ability to be put on some kind of farm team where a measure of perseverance plus noticeable writing talent will give you a chance for the big leagues.

There are about two hundred production companies who are likely to sell made-for-TV movies to a network, so you have a wide choice to send material to. Using an agent will improve your chances, but if you have a sample script and some fresh, intelligent, timely concepts, you may be able to go straight to one of these companies.

Soap Operas

They started on the radio or, if you want to be academic about it, in Victorian magazines where writers as exalted as Dickens serialized their gargantuan novels. They are the absolute staple of daytime television. In the eighties, in the filmed episodic genre, they were big at night as well, in the guise of such shows as "Dallas," "Dynasty" and "Falcon Crest," big budget, 35mm shows with different demands. The soap operas I now am referring to are the likes of "General Hospital," "Santa Barbara," "One Life to Live," and so forth.

The soaps employ teams of writers, usually known as associate writers, and a head writer who pulls it all together and runs the vital script conferencing. Many of the writers work at home, but their work schedule runs roughly fifty weeks a year. They are experienced and sometimes move from one show to another. Breaking in is *not* easy. One of the best ways to do it is to know someone on the inside, or to write whole episodes and give them to an agent specializing in the field. It pays well but is very demanding, involving complete adherence to an agreed upon plot structure and line of characterization.

Other Fiction

The miniseries genre started in the seventies on network television with *Roots* and *Rich Man, Poor Man*. Both of those groundbreakers came from successful popular novels, and the trend has continued since. The networks like to draw material from massively successful writers like Jackie Collins. The author of the book is in the running to write the teleplay, though writing the actual script is usually not her job. In most cases, a very experienced TV writer is brought in—these series are far too expensive and ratings-hungry to risk much hiring of newcomers. The best thing to do if you want to write a miniseries is to watch and absorb as many of them as you can and learn the tricks of the trade.

The onetime drama special resembles feature film work in that it comes from the same source—a one-shot idea that has inescapable appeal. It is more the province of pay-per-view cable TV (Home Box Office, Showtime, etc.) and PBS than network TV. Having an agent is almost essential to get one of these sold, no matter how good it is. In the case of PBS, there is always the chance that an executive at "American Playhouse" or some other series show (see the interview with Lynne Doherty) will take a fancy to your finished script and hire you to develop the teleplay, but even there, given the limited number of TV spots available, an agent would be more than useful.

I include feature movies only because the 1980s introduced the onslaught of pay-per-view cable TV and home video rental. Writing a movie for the theaters these days is often the equivalent of doing a TV movie. All films, no matter how successful in the theaters, eventually end up on cable or in the video store, so in a sense all movies are made for television.

Some lower budget efforts are thought of primarily as cable and rental items because of their marginal chances of success in the cinema. Deals can be made because of the ancillary monies to come from features destined for cable, rental and foreign markets, both theatrical and for television.

Can It Be Done?

There is an expanded market nowadays for TV writing. This improves your general chances of getting work and finding homes for your worked out fantasies and concepts. The new markets do not provide new employment opportunities in themselves — much of the writing is still done by accepted, proven professionals. They do encourage lower budgets and experimentation with new writers who will work for far less than their network and feature co-workers.

There are ways to get into the fiction writing profession, but it is not a cakewalk. We can write, we have good ideas, we are in touch with current trends in TV — but the problem is that we are dealing with an industry infrastructure where dollars determine decision making.

The way to handle it is to remain optimistic and realistic and to coolly calculate how to break the code. Fiction is easier to write than it is to sell. Your personal objective should be to write every day, get your work to someone whose judgment you trust, and then after good feedback get it to someone who has some leverage power. It is a frustrating task, but with determination it can be done.

Chapter Six:

NONFICTION:
THE ART
OF THE
PROPOSAL

NONFICTION FILM AND VIDEO HAVE CHANGED IN THE LAST FEW years. At one time it was hardly considered the province of the writer. Now the form has expanded to the point where the narrative component is an integral part of the overall gestalt.

Changes in the Nonfiction Form

When documentaries were a relatively obscure genre in the tradition of Flaherty and Grierson, it was almost thought to be heresy to supplement the edited footage with explicatory voice-overs. Then, by the 1970s, broadcast television had cultivated the documentary as a valid and even commercial entity that needed to present as much information as quickly and compactly as possible. By that time, TV documentaries were covering an awesome range of subjects, and the added narration became accepted. Documentaries became the province of the television news department as well as the dedicated and serious-minded independent producer.

Now the genre is multifaceted and has become a recognizable part of the television programming spectrum. The magazine show — a popularized, segmented evolution of the documentary — even has ratings successes, frequently in the guise of huge TV hits like CBS's "60 Minutes" and ABC's "20/20," where hosts and correspondents write their voice-overs very carefully so as to transmit the maximum amount of information or to give the piece a specific slant, something the traditional documentarian might find offensive.

This kind of programming started in England in the late fifties with Richard Dimbleby's "Panorama," later transmuted into a precursor of tabloid television with British commercial television's "World in Action" and "This Week." The first regular American news and news feature magazine show was PBS's "Great American Dream Machine," which I co-created with Al Perlmutter and Jack Willis in the early seventies.

Independent Productions

There are far fewer "rules" on how to pitch and sell this kind of television as compared with fiction television. The business of nonfiction TV is not in the same league as that of TV drama: There isn't as much money to be made; there aren't as many outlets; it isn't as glamorous or as secure, even after you have had a few successful films or tapes produced and broadcast. Also, the majority of writing jobs are just that—assignments rather than original efforts. You work for a TV station or network, and they assign the particular job to you. Let's put that aside for the moment and discuss independent writing.

Let's say you have an idea for a piece, and you are collaborating with a producer or you are a "hyphenate"—a producer-writer or a producer-director-writer. Where do you take your idea for financing and what do you have to show in order to stand any chance of getting some financing to do the project? The truth is—yet again—not an easy one to contemplate. Without a track record it isn't easy to get development money. Usually you have to do some of the shooting and writing before any money person or television station or granting body will give you any significant money.

Typical Situations

A typical situation goes like this: You arrive at an idea you feel passionately about. You write it up. You try to get money. You are told that you have to present some evidence that you are competent and visionary enough to deliver a finished product. The best way through all this is to write a convincing, committed proposal. There just isn't any way around this. Then you have to research what kind of entity is likely to be at least interested in the idea. Public broadcasting is one obvious medium. PBS itself might be interested or CPB (the Corporation for Public Broadcasting) in Washington. The National Endowment for the Humanities is another likely place, or the Rockefeller or Ford Foundations. A localized group like the New York State Council on the Arts or its equivalent in your state, if there is one, might be a good place to go.

One of the best ways to find out is to carefully check out the credits at the beginning or end of the documentaries on public television. Try to approach the group that has funded a documentary similar to yours. Keep in mind the concept of joint funding or "step deals," where you are able to get a development grant, then production and shooting money, and finally post-production funding. It is always to your advantage to scrape together some money to do some initial shooting to show your prospective financiers.

Structuring a Proposal

Designing a proposal for a nonfiction project remains a personal matter as agents and producers have no exact expectations. Foundations that grant money sometimes require the requester to fill in standard forms that are self-explanatory. But if there is no form, then what I will suggest covers all the necessary segments in a logical order. Your project might demand a different emphasis, but my model should help you organize your thoughts.

First, a "table of contents" to give you an overall view of what your proposal should include:

1. Rationale
2. General introduction
3. Film or tape structure/outline
4. Budget
5. Narration model

6. Personnel
7. Credits/résumés
8. Distribution aims
9. Background materials
10. Conclusion

A proposal should be more than five pages and, in most cases, fewer than twenty-five pages long. More than anything it should show two aspects of your professional character: that you are firmly in control of the project and that you are passionate about it.

Rationale

I made this category up a few years ago when I realized that most prospective funders and producers need to know right up front what is the rationale behind the proposed film or videotape. What is so incredibly important that they should invest sizable amounts of money in something that might make a small profit, might break even, but most likely will result in some kind of loss? The main point to get across is that the film will enlighten, educate and entertain even if it doesn't make a fortune—though you should never even suggest that it won't make money. If you have your business wits about you, it should do well, particularly if it is not ultra-esoteric and personal and it relates to a wide range of viewers.

In this first and most imprinting of sections, you should clearly state why the film should be made and why it hasn't been made before. You should make a strong statement about its social purpose while stressing its viewer appeal.

If you were proposing a piece about, say, rap music in New York City, you would start by briefly telling the reader what rap music is and then quickly explaining why this particular documentary has a unique viewpoint, like no other television piece that has gone before it. Something like this:

"Rap music is a genuine inner city art form, based on the rhythms of modern black music while employing a subtle and dynamic poetic form. It actually originated as Jamaican "toast" poetry, a lilting, spoken mutation of reggae music. It is one of the most popular and accepted forms of late twentieth-century urban expression. Although there have been television reports on the music, no one has yet attempted to show the form as it is from the streets, tracing its history and covering all its variations, with a narration based on the work of leading rappers. The time is right for an in-depth look at this growing popular reflection of today's city rhythms, and "All Around Rap" will do this for a wide audience. This film should be made right now because, not only will it be entertaining, but it will give real insight into a music which the majority of the population know very little about. "All Around Rap" will be a visual and musical aid to bringing the races a little closer together."

Some prospective executive producers are so busy (or like to think they should be) that if the opening of a proposal doesn't get to it right away, they almost feel duty bound to put the sheaf of dot matrix covered papers aside and wait for another time to look at it. Stimulate them right away. Don't even give them a chance to dismiss you because they don't immediately know what they're in for. If they don't like it, then so be it. They would not have liked it in any case. If they agree with your rationale—which is my shorthand for "why this film should be made"—then they will read the rest of the proposal with some interest, already basically on your side. Your skills as a writer start right here.

General Introduction

You should use this section to give some background on the subject and start to show how it would be documented. This is the place to write anything you want about the passion behind the film. If appropriate, this is the time to go into the history of the subject, where it fits into the overall social and cultural fabric of the day, and what your individual perspective on it is. In a proposal I did for a documentary about the Israeli/Palestinian conflict (called "The Road to Peace") I used this part of the document to relate a capsule history of the conflict—not too lengthy (this was not an academic tome) but enough to show that I knew what I was talking about and also for the reader to brush up on general knowledge of the matter at hand.

In the case of our mythical documentary about rap music, it would be fine at this point to talk about the history of inner city American music; its relationship to rhythm and blues and to the original blues; its basic message or messages; the misconceptions about its so-called violent content; its wider ramifications both in the ghetto and in the overall cultural and commercial scene. Never get too esoteric, or the reader will subliminally feel that the film may be too obscure or highbrow and that possibly no one will feel the urge to distribute it, let alone watch it on television where it will compete with other programming much easier to absorb after a hard day's work.

Of course, all of this pragmatic marketing advice applies only if you want to eventually get this on broadcast television. If the intention is to make a 100 percent pure film that will emerge at documentary festivals and the like, then any dilution or intellectual compromise may not be to your taste.

It is beneficial to let people know whether films or tapes of this kind have been made before and to list them, so that your readers know that you know. This is one of the ways in which you can show that you are in control and that you have knowledge not only in the subject to be filmed but also in the gestation of media coverage of it.

This introductory section can be used for almost anything in and around the content, keeping away from aspects to be covered later in the proposal.

Outline

This is where your professionalism genuinely starts to show. You should state categorically at this point what format you plan to shoot in: videotape (1-inch, ¼-inch, Beta, Beta SP, Super Eight, High Eight) or film (16mm, Super Sixteen, 35mm) or a combination of the two. It should also be stated what the final product will be mastered in—usually 1-inch video these days. Then, to the best of your ability, you should outline the documentary. Much will depend on what "actuality" occurs in front of the camera—which can hardly be predicted in all but the most orchestrated of programs—but you should have a good idea of what you want. The overall shape of the film should be shown, allowing the reader of the proposal a good idea of what the final product will be. The desired length should also be revealed in this section. The main thing is to prove that you know what you are aiming for. Back to the rap show:

1. Rap song done out in the street
2. Rapper talking about when he first started
3. Film collage of city streets with rap song as track
4. Archival footage of rhythm and blues from the forties
5. Middle-class male asking about the music
6. Sophisticated music video of rap song
7. Reggae toasting song
8. Young teenager doing his own form of rap

And so on, going from beginning to end. If you feel that it is more revealing, then you can go into greater depth within each program element, remembering though that much of this structure will come out of editing. It is unwise to suggest that you know exactly what each segment will contain when so much will depend on what happens extemporaneously at the time of shooting. The key factor is your showing that you have a definite vision in your head of what you want to capture and you know how you will sculpt the raw footage once you have it.

Budget

This should be as detailed as you can make it. It is extremely important that the budget be as accurate as possible. It is tempting to think that a funding source could not possibly know the ins and outs of budgeting, and this may be true in most cases, but the figures should be within 5 or 10 percent accuracy so that *you* will not be wiped out halfway through the production because you didn't ask for enough money. Divide the budget into preproduction, shooting, and post-production; include travel, accommodation, insurance, catering, graphics, sound mixing, music rights, announcer fees, producer/director/writer fees, and so on.

Add a 10 percent contingency fee at the end to protect yourself from unknowns. Don't pad a budget too much. Conversely, don't skimp, or inevitably there will be problems down the line.

Narration Model

From the writer's point of view, this is the most interesting section, but actually given the normal process of documentary film or tape making, it is the least predictable, unless you are making a very formal film that doesn't rely on unpredictable actuality. Even if you have no idea what the exact nature of the final product will be, you should be able to suggest the kind of narration you want. As long as you make it clear in this section that that is all you can reasonably do, it is fine to create some sort of paradigm. In our rap film, you might do something of this order:

In the opening sequence, the voice-over will be a mixture of explanatory narration and bits and pieces of rap songs by the rappers spotlighted in the rest of the piece, starting with "Rap cannot be pinned down . . . it comes out of everyday speech and is not a written form . . . it seems ridiculous to even say what it is . . . like the words of the street, it changes almost every day — INSERT here a piece of relevant rap — here's the recent words of Streetmaster King Ice. . . ."

Give at least the opening words and then something from the middle and a little from the end. At least this will give the proposal reader some idea of what it will sound like. It is more documented proof that you have the whole work in your mind and that you are working toward a clear end, no matter what comes up on the film. You know what the final film should be like, and you probably won't blow all the money on an endless amount of footage going nowhere. It is a rare documentary that emanates from a written piece, but that is never out of the question. Maybe that will be your way of doing it. Obviously, if you have written the entire voice-over and you are shooting footage to correspond to it, this section of the proposal has increased significance. You might want to print the whole thing in that case, giving the reader a real idea of the progression of your movie.

Personnel

This is a list of the people who will actually make the film. The producer, director, writer, editor, and narrator would be the most important personnel to present. You might write a paragraph or two saying why this group of professionals is especially good for this project, given their background and personal interests and expertise. It should fit on one page if possible.

Credits/Résumés

Briefly list your group's main credits, particularly as they relate to your own project. If the film's logistics are complicated, then you should also include the production manager, who will be the one taking care of that end of the process.

Distribution Aims

Discuss in this section where you want to place the program. If you have already received some tentative affirmative responses, make a big thing of it here. If there has been some sort of letter of agreement or statement of interest pending the completion of the piece, include a copy of the letter or letters. If you have not yet reached this point, make sure you have some sort of plan, even if it is pure speculation — PBS or Channel 4 in Britain or whatever. Also, if appropriate, mention the possibility of home video sales and placement in educational institutions like libraries or universities. All of this is grist for the mill of a successful pitch at the proposal level. Be careful not to be outlandish in your aspirations. Don't simply list all the outlets you can think of — it gives you the persona of a dreamer, and that is the last impression you want to give.

Background Materials

This is the place to put any articles you feel would add to the understanding of the content plus any letters of approval by relevant people or institutions. In our hypothetical rap film, it would be beneficial to include letters of agreement from any performers you wanted in the film. Even if the funder or prospective executive producer does not feel the need to read much of this, it is still smart to include any of this kind of material just to create a perception of thoroughness on your part. Much of this seems to be a touch pretentious, but I assure you it helps when people are risking real money. They always want to feel that you are completely on top of your subject.

Conclusion

In the conclusion, sum up your aims for the movie and some of the ramifications of making it—what it will add to public knowledge of the subject, what its "shelf life" might be, how crucial it is to further understanding, the exact focus it will bring, and why you think it should be made now rather than at any other time. There is no need to make this last section too long, as you have already covered in some detail everything about the making of the film and you don't want to repeat yourself.

Staple the pages together neatly and put the whole thing in a plastic binder. As a final check, make sure that the layout and overall appearance are good, then send it off and be satisfied that you have represented yourself admirably. If you like, you can show it to friends or professional colleagues for some useful feedback, but don't agonize too much over it—the main point is to get it out and start the ball rolling so that you can get down to actually making the film.

The Compleat Beatles

Nonfiction television is not the staple of broadcast television except as regular TV news, both local and network. Therefore, it has not engendered a formulaic approach to backing, except that the funders in the United States who attract regular entreaties and proposals for partial or total funding are well known. This has created an ad hoc approach. Just giving a few examples from personal experience will demonstrate.

The Compleat Beatles was a two-hour film created for MGM/ United Artists in 1982. I was brought in as the writer some months after the project was initiated by a small New York production company called Delilah Films, a subsidiary of a book publisher called Delilah Books, which specialized in music books.

The evolution of the project went like this: *The Compleat Beatles*, the first completely accurate transcription of all of the Beatles' songs, was published. It also had some text and many photographs. EMI in England decided they wanted to create a short commercial to promote the book on both sides of the Atlantic. Patrick Montgomery, a film director and owner of Archive Productions, was hired to make this short commercial. Patrick got the job for two main reasons. He had proven himself a fine director with a film biography of Eric Von Stroheim, the distinguished director and actor from the early period of moviemaking. Also, Archive Productions, as the name suggests, is one of the leading archival film collectors in the United States. Patrick had quick access to much of the Beatles footage. EMI actually owned much of this film. Lord Grade, then head of EMI, was so impressed by Patrick's small film collage that he commissioned Patrick and Delilah to produce a full-length "biopic" of the Beatles. As you can well imagine, this was a juicy project, as no one up to that time had been able to gain licensed access to the bulk of the footage. Patrick proceeded to put as much film together as he could, tracing it from all over the world. Several writers were given the formidable task of writing the narrative voice-over. None of them was able to come up with the exact tone and style that he wanted, and eventually Patrick came to me.

As an Englishman living in the United States, I was exactly what they wanted; the film had to appeal to an American audience first, designed as it was for both theatrical and home video distribution. Added to that, my mother's family hailed from Liverpool, the home of the Beatles, so I had some firsthand knowledge of their roots.

I was invited to Patrick's offices on West Twenty-fifth Street in New York City, where I was shown some of the footage. Patrick asked me to look carefully at about ten minutes of roughly edited film and then take a quick shot at writing some narration. To my everlasting surprise, I was given the job the next day. Eighteen months later, my narration was completed and recorded for the movie track by the English actor, Malcolm McDowell.

This was the way it came about. No proposals, just the concatenation of circumstances and a fast test of my ability to create the right set of words to go over film of the Fab Four. So this was a classic case of assignment. The film was not my idea, and even the way it had to be written came from the mind of the director, Patrick Montgomery. It was one of the most exciting and satisfying jobs imaginable; I was responsible for helping to create a film time capsule about one of the most fascinating phenomena of our times. Everybody knew something about the Beatles, so I had to be both accurate and novel.

The only "pitching" I did was in the form of writing the best ten minutes of narration I was capable of on that warm New York afternoon on Twenty-fifth Street.

Other Examples

A completely different example would be my work on a syndicated documentary called "Women Under Cover" in 1989. Tim Snow, the producer, and I wrote ten pages of proposal to convince an independent executive producer to come up with seed money to start shooting. The show was about three female undercover narcotics agents in New York City and Miami. I based my hypothetical example for an episodic show, "Donna West, D.E.A.," on this real-life experience. In this case it was a gradual funding process, with writing an essential element all through. The voice-over, written for the "Hill Street Blues" star Betty Thomas, was created after watching raw footage; the final narration, after watching film that was fine edited. The words, though, were an essential part of the gradual gathering of money to finish the project. So this show came out of a collaboration in proposal writing between a producer and a writer, with advice from undercover police and D.E.A. officials along the way.

In 1975, I wrote a proposal for the Rockefeller Foundation for a series to be called "Video and Television Review," otherwise known as "VTR." It was for an open-ended series to be shown on public television, coming out of WNET-TV, Channel 13, in New York City. I had to explain carefully that it was to be a weekly showcase for the new breed of video artists. I was at the time one of the artists-in-residence at the Television Laboratory at Channel 13. Because of that position, the proposal did not come out of the blue, but I still had to prove to the wily folks at Rockefeller that it was a project worth funding.

The proposal was about twenty-five pages long and followed the guidelines I spoke of above. Because I was not sure what each artist would do, it was necessary to show preknowledge of intent rather than details. My main aim was to prove the need for a program of this type at a time when video technology, in the form of newly invented synthesizers and other video enhancing technology, was making great leaps forward. Because I was asking for a relatively large amount, I could not be slipshod or superficial in describing the basic outline of the series. I stated as clearly as I could what would be the likely content of the series overall and how much it would cost within a margin of plus or minus 10 percent.

It worked. The series went on the air in 1975 and survived in one form or another for many years. It involved dozens of artists and hundreds of thousands of Rockefeller dollars. It stands as a good example of how to get an idea across without actually knowing the details of what was to appear on the air. I have to emphasize again that it succeeded in garnering the necessary money because I knew, before I wrote the proposal, exactly what I wanted. There were no big gaps in my vision. And I showed strong enthusiasm—even passion—in the words I chose to describe the series. I made a powerful case for the need to give these innovative, often quite brilliant, video artists a broadcast television outlet.

For every successful proposal I've written, there have been several that flopped. Some of these were duds, not because the proposals lacked quality but because the timing was not right or the projects were too expensive or something similar had already been produced. But I have to admit, failure was occasionally the result of a badly aimed piece of begging or plain bad writing. I remember doing one for the Rockefeller Foundation in the mid-seventies asking for backing for a series about meditation. They turned it down not only because they didn't think the idea was the kind of thing they wanted to put money into, but also, I later gleaned, because the way I described the project was far too esoteric. I rambled on about representing visualization techniques with various spectacular video effects and actually talking the viewer through these experiences with a seductive, hypnotic voice-over. Unfortunately, hapless viewers could have either watched the video effects or listened to the announcer speaking — they couldn't do both, and to do them at separate times would have made the show far too cumbersome and ultimately utterly boring to anyone not going through the meditation. It might have proved interesting later to a buyer in the days of home video, but I can't attest to that. Even if the idea could have been salvaged, the way I described it in the proposal made too many assumptions about the reader, let alone the viewer. The timing was bad, but the proposal was worse.

Another time, I proposed a TV biography about the visionary inventor of alternating current, Nicola Tesla, but I simply hadn't done enough research at that time to convince anyone that I knew enough about the genius — it was quite obvious I hadn't studied too assiduously. This is not to say that the idea itself was a bad one — just that the proposal was too thin in its presentation of probable content. I intend to try that one again when I have the time to do the right kind of research. Sometimes the concept itself has little worth, but more often than not, the problem is in the proposal.

The best test for the directness of proposal writing I have ever had was in the co-writing with my colleague Marty Perlmutter of a proposal for a Video Art Anthology for Pioneer, which is a Japanese company. In order to impress on the executives at Pioneer in Tokyo that they really should fork out twenty million yen to anthologize American video artists on laserdisc, we had to write a proposal that not only was solidly communicative in English but would survive their Japanese translator. To ensure that this would happen we had to know: exactly what we wanted; how much it would cost; how long it would take to produce; how many laserdiscs it would fit on; why it would appeal first and foremost to the Japanese market; why we were the only ones who could do it; what would be the nature of the narration; who would do it; how that would be done in both English and Japanese; whether the small American laserdisc market would be interested in it; and more. This was not an easy task, but we wrote the proposal without frills, answering these questions as succinctly as possible and being razor sharp on budget details and the time needed to put it together. We got the money. The double laserdisc was released in Japan in the summer of 1988 with both Japanese and English voice-overs, the latter of which I did myself in New York City. It was something of a coup, and it could not have happened if Perlmutter and I had not made the proposal conform precisely to our original vision. The Japanese expect the letter of the law in execution, so we had to make the document represent as accurately as possible what we would in fact end up doing. It was a supremely good test of proposal writing.

Write your proposal so it mirrors your concept, represents the most accurate possible version of the production process, and allows you enough leeway to make the best television show you can after the money has been granted. Honesty and sharp focus are the two qualities to aim for.

Chapter Seven:
NONFICTION GENRES

NONFICTION TELEVISION IS WIDENING ITS RANGE IN THE 1990s, mainly because of the increased amount of air time available via cable TV and the vastly enlarged universe of home video. By 1990, shows like "60 Minutes," "20/20," "48 Hours," and "PrimeTime Live" had become consistent ratings successes on network television. This has made the whole nonfiction field more attractive for the people with the money.

Nonfiction television is far less structured than fiction. With a single-minded attitude and a working knowledge of the real needs of television programmers, you can get ahead. Writers who want to be involved in nonfiction television are a rare breed; the actual writing is usually far less challenging to the imagination because you are mainly doing voice-over narration. Much of the writing effort actually goes into preparing the text for a proposal, the main part of which will never appear in the program. Nevertheless, the proposal writing should be as good as possible to impress potential buyers that you are articulate and know your subject extremely well.

Documentary

Documentary is something of a generic term these days. In strict terms it means a film or tape that is based on the truth, actuality, the facts as they are recorded of an event or a continuing set of events. The distinguished documentarian Frederick Wiseman makes strictly "pure" films for which he overshoots and then does meticulous editing. At the other end of the spectrum would be syndicated television shows that might re-create events or do formal interviews to get a certain point of view across. In general though, the modern documentary takes a subject, shoots the heck out of it, and then is fashioned through editing into something that will hold viewers. Writing proposals is the mainstay of funding these kinds of films.

"Writing a documentary" is something of a contradiction in terms, because what happens in front of the camera creates its own contours in the final film or tape. In many cases, however, a voice-over is necessary to give the film extra depth and make it more accessible.

The process goes like this: You think of the idea and get the money to film or tape the material. Then you do a rough edit of some kind (sometimes referred to as an "off-line" edit), followed by a polished (or "on-line") edit. Somewhere in the latter stages of rough editing, the narration begins to take form. Then as the final edit is done, the writing is made to fit exactly and move the flow of the film along. By the time of the *final* final edit, the narration is recorded by your chosen announcer or commentator.

Sometimes the financing will come early on, occasionally before even one word is written, if the film's quality speaks for itself. In other cases, you may not get any money until there is some kind of rough voice-over. And more often than not, the real money comes when you have finalized the piece. Documentary film and tape making, then, is largely speculative and demands some kind of private backing. Nevertheless, the skills of the writer are often crucial to the success of the piece. In the classic Flaherty, Wiseman, Pennebaker tradition of 16mm filmmaking, the voice-over was a last resort, but nowadays, the form has evolved and often demands some very good writing.

The prerequisite is that you as writer or writer/director or writer/producer, depending on where you sit in the project, have a real passion for the subject and know what you are embarking upon. Sometimes you know very little before the actual filming, but in the main, the writer has a good knowledge of what the film will be about before he even writes the proposal.

Selling it depends on many factors. Sometimes an interested party will put up the money from just a spoken concept (very rare), but usually you need at least a few pages of clearly written explication of what you want to do. PBS and local educational stations do buy documentaries, but they are reluctant to put up the money until there is some kind of evidence that the film is in the process of being made. Then they will put in the bucks to do post-production (editing, graphics, final master print or tape, sound mixing, special effects). Documentaries do not usually make any money, so most filmmakers are happy to get help with the production and some kind of fee for airing. The speed of interest in acquiring or finishing the production of a documentary often depends on your track record in the field, so if you are a beginner, you have to prove yourself.

Biography

This is a subform of documentary, dealing in depth with someone's life story gathered from interviews, archival footage, newspaper articles and the like. Sometimes it is composed just of factual material; sometimes it has a docu-drama form, which involves re-creation/dramatization of events in the person's life. Either of these forms presents a good opportunity for the serious writer. Narration is normally crucial to this kind of documentary. The "rules" of documentary selling I have already dealt with apply to this form also. It is a satisfying writing job because it allows the writer to take real events of the past and translate them into a compelling continuum. If you have a driving need to write one of these biographies, then you have to acquire rights to a book or put the research together yourself—a big job. Usually, this kind of work is done by assignment, but occasionally someone puts the effort into making an independent film or tape and sells it.

Musical Biography

Since the rise of MTV and the music video, there is far more product involving music, particularly rock and roll music, but also jazz and classical. Public television in particular has been involved in making many musical biographies. The popularity of the form revolves around the public fascination with the lives behind the notes and lyrics of famous musicians.

The long-form musical biography, like my own *The Compleat Beatles*, is expensive to make and often presents a tremendous problem in rights acquisition, but the expansion of video distribution forms has made it possible for these shows to actually get produced. It is almost impossible to produce a musical biography without the backing of a major production group, mainly because the "sync license" fees and lawyers' fees involved are prohibitive. However, if you write something outstanding, shop it around; there may be a great deal of commercial value to the work and it could get done.

The main thing to remember about nonfiction television in general, not just biographical video, is that it requires essentially a team effort, and the film will simply not get off the ground unless a producer, director, writer, editor and perhaps others work together—and this almost always demands lots of money. Private backing is the most likely way to get this kind of television produced.

Commercial Feature News

If you want to write for feature news, you have to attach yourself to—get a staff job on—one of the news magazine shows on network, syndicated, or public television. Most of these shows these days are hardly definable as news at all. They include "soft" features, mainly about "lifestyle" subjects, and entertainment coverage—celebrities, sports people and public figures. Getting a job on one of these shows is certainly pursuing your desire to be a writer, but it is more like writing advertising copy in that you are usually dealing with very short segments, where the information has to be compressed into tiny, condensed "soundbites."

This category does not truly fit within the parameters of this book, but I wanted to at least mention it to give you some idea of the scope of nonfiction writing for television. The only way to enter this branch of the profession is to contact the networks, the production companies or the individual stations, public or commercial, that produce these shows. "20/20" and shows like it do bring in new people every so often, but you would need some background in the field, even in the production end, to be seriously considered. It is a legitimate place to go, but it is not a place to imagine yourself doing in-depth, creative writing. It's a job and can earn you good money. Try for it if you are extremely attracted to this brand of television. Otherwise, leave it alone.

Nature Programs

Look to PBS and the basic cable (the kind that comes as part of the package on most cable systems, unlike HBO or Showtime, for which you pay extra) for this kind of programming. Suffice to say that this is usually staff work. I feel this programming has increasing importance in a world where ecology and the threatened environment have become everyday news topics. Many people are now passionate about these nature-oriented issues, so it is natural that more and more artists will start writing about them, just to add their consciousness to the public awareness. If you have written something extraordinary about the natural world, then I would advise you—or your agent if you have one—to contact the people at "Nova" at WGBH-TV in Boston or the very open-minded programming people at the Discovery Channel. It is a hopeful sign of the times that there are outlets for a kind of writing that would have been considered totally esoteric a few years ago.

How-to

This area of nonfiction includes health, diet, exercise and fitness films. The advent of home video and the massive rental business around it has introduced a new type of television to the American public—the repeatable tape which you can watch enough times to actually learn how to do something. These tapes are often produced by major concerns like Lorimar (who did the enormously successful *Jane Fonda Workout* tapes). If they are low-budget efforts, however, they are frequently produced by small production companies. They do not always include any narration—the exposition speaks for itself—but occasionally they do.

I wrote one how-to program called *Balletics* a few years ago that presented an exercise technique using modified ballet practice to tone the body. It actually demanded quite a bit of voice-over explanation, and I wrote it in collaboration with a noted ballet teacher and the tape's producer. I was paid a decent sum to do it, and the gig came from a producer I had worked with before. It did not take that much work and is a reasonable quality production. If you have an idea for a tape of this genre, then it might be worth your while to pitch it to a small company, keeping in mind a rough budget.

Fine Arts

The expansion of video distribution systems makes a tape about the fine arts much more of a possibility now. PBS, the Discovery Channel and maybe the Arts and Entertainment Channel (the latter two basic cable systems) are good outlets for this kind of video. Usually, foundations and federal granting bodies like the National Endowment for the Arts and the National Endowment for the Humanities are the places to go for this kind of programming. It is not at all inappropriate for a writer to chase down this kind of money because much of the work involves a strong narrative line. This is where you might be wearing the two hats of writer *and* producer. If the subject is commercial enough you might even try to interest sources of independent funding, like a venture capital group of investors.

Conclusion

Nonfiction television has expanded greatly in the last few years to include much more popular forms of programming (shows such as "Inside Edition" and "The Reporters" as well as the more generic "evening magazine" type of series). Writers should take heart to see that their craft is more and more essential to keep the TV machine operating.

Chapter Eight:

WORKING
WITH AGENTS
AND PRODUCERS

ALL WELL AND GOOD," I HEAR YOU SAYING, "ALL THIS LOFTY
advice about agents and complex proposals and formatting
screenplays . . . but how do I actually start? What's my first move?
What kind of language should I use when I talk on the phone to
these high-powered folks in New York City and Los Angeles? Is
it really plausible that I can break into this world? I don't sit by
the swimming pool jabbering into my portable phone with my
state-of-the-art laptop computer on my knees while my secretary
brings me an endless alternating stream of correspondence and
banana margaritas. I'm just ordinary people. Is this all a pipe
dream? Should I just get real and go back to typing school?"

How Do You Start?

These are good questions. There is no harm in trying to be calm
and detached about your aspirations to work in television. Television professionals are only human, nothing magical, nothing of
the Nietzchean superman or superwoman about them. They had
the same insecurities about themselves as you do. Many of them
still do. It is all a question of how much you want to do this,
whether you are willing to take the plunge and believe in yourself,
and ultimately, whether you have the goods.

When you are satisfied that you have something very special

that you can visualize on the television screen, then you have to decide how much of this you can really do alone. Maybe you are the kind of person who does not need to use a broker of some kind to communicate your talents and distribute your writing to those who need to see it. I warn you that even if you have this singular kind of self-confidence, the industry may not care. It's like aspiring to be a soldier but not wanting to join the army. Yes, Rambo pulled it off, but he may be the only one and he wasn't even real.

The better your work, the more you should think about quality representation. Then you stand a better chance of being taken seriously. Even if you work with the nonfiction group, you'll need someone to advise you on fees, royalties and the like.

The First Phone Call

Let's get down to basics. If you have written a fiction piece of any type, you need to communicate with an agent or a producer or at least make some kind of contact. This means there has to be an initial phone call. Who do you make it to and what do you say? Let's start with calling an agency. You have already done some research and found out which agent or agency seems to fit your bill. Call up and ask for this agent's secretary or assistant. Here's a make-believe conversation that would be the right way to go:

RECEPTIONIST: Hello, Beresford and Smythe Agency. Can I help you?

YOU: Yes. My name is Jim Blanding and I would like to talk with Joe Weinstein's office.

RECEPTIONIST: Okay, sir, I'll put you through. Hold on, please. . . . (holding) . . .

SECRETARY: Good morning, Mr. Weinstein's office. Can I help you?

YOU: Yes. My name is Jim Blanding and I am interested in representation. I have written a screenplay for television. Can you tell me how I should proceed?

SECRETARY: Have you worked with us before?

YOU: No.

SECRETARY: Well then, I would suggest you write a letter to Mr. Weinstein, telling him what you want and including a small outline of what your script's about. . . . Oh, and include a résumé. Okay?

YOU: Yes, fine. Thank you very much.

There is a 99 percent probability that this is how the initial conversation will flow. So that's out of the way. Nothing too horrific about that. This is the accepted procedure, and no matter how world-shattering you feel your script actually is, this is still the only way to go when approaching a busy agent. To be any pushier will almost certainly lead to a bad impression from the start and simply cannot do you any good in the short or long run.

Then send your query letter, following the guidelines in chapter four. Your job after this is to be patient. Most agents will read it or have an assistant read it first, and if it strikes their fancy they will reply positively. It may take a month or more. If they don't like it, they may tell you why and this could be valuable information. Of course, if you don't agree, you can continue pitching it without any changes.

Just make sure that you are not ignoring feedback that could help your script turn a corner. The common myth is that agents are jaded. Some of them are, but my experience tells me that they are willing to put out the energy to help a good writer improve his or her work. After all, you could end up earning money for them. They need new clients, even if they are already successful agents.

The Résumé

Now, going into reverse a little, the agent's secretary asked you for a résumé. Do you have one? Or do you feel that there simply isn't enough stuff to write down? This is a common paranoia. Sometimes writers do come right out of nowhere and have never done anything relevant before that would be useful for a résumé, but most beginning writers have done enough to warrant at least a page. It does not all have to be related to writing television scripts. I am not in favor of listing completely irrelevant jobs like being a waiter or driving a cab, no matter how honorable those jobs are. No agent or producer will, in truth, care in the least. But make sure you include any student writing assignments or film school experience and anything that you got paid for, no matter how lowly. If you have any broadcast credits, even if they are in production rather than writing, include them and give full details of who they were for, when they were done, and where the show you worked on was broadcast.

Meeting With an Agent

If the agent likes the piece, she will want to arrange a meeting. You should expedite this with one more phone call, if she wrote in response. She may have called you herself and that would probably result in a meeting. If you live a distance away from her office, arrange your visit so you give yourself a little extra time to travel and then go.

Don't worry too much about the way you look—the agent's interest is in your writing, not in your sense of fashion, but try to be neat. Everything you bring to bear upon these initial encounters with "the biz" can help you. Be on time, even though you will probably have to wait. Agents are always on the phone. Try not to be nervous. She has already stated she likes your work. You're in good shape.

It's a good idea to be friendly with everyone you meet before the boss gets to you—the receptionist, the secretary, or her assistant—they can be invaluable to you down the line. If they like you, they can make life a lot easier later when you need a quick answer or some help dealing with the bureaucracy. I'm not saying be false or smarmy, just be nice—it's worth it.

When you do finally get in the office, be sure to listen to her before you launch into any grand orations about yourself or your work. She is on your side; anything she says will be useful to you. Don't be put off by a constant stream of interrupting phone calls—an agent's main tool of communication is the telephone, and few have the time to stop all calls, although some agents will do that even for a beginning writer. Keep your more extravagant expectations at a minimum—although this may not be a false start, there may be a long way to go before you will see any big action. You have succeeded in getting through to the agent, but she now has the task of persuading others, the ones who must lay out real money, rather than just time or energy. She will likely recommend some critical corrections and have suggestions as to where the script would receive a decent hearing.

An agent, if he is any good at all, has many clients, and may not make you a priority case unless the script is so obviously timely that he feels immediate action is necessary. My experience with a big agency was that my first agent showed a great deal of liking for my work but unfortunately never got round to really pushing it—he was just too busy. Sometimes it is better to find a less prominent agent who can concentrate more on new writers, not being constantly preoccupied with his bigger clients. This is a judgment call, and only you can ascertain whether you are being dealt with fairly or being left on the shelf until someone asks him if he has anything that approximates your script. Whatever you decide, be sure to give whoever you choose enough time to move on it.

Although dealing with a producer directly requires a different approach, essentially the same sequence of events will take place. It may seem a more direct route to deal straightaway with a producer, but unless he is dripping with money, he also must prove to someone else that this script is worth developing and producing. Patience, patience, patience.

Difficulties and Dilemmas

I want to discuss what might happen in a meeting with a producer once you have had the invigorating experience of initial acceptance. I think it's most useful to imagine a situation that presents difficulties and dilemmas to you. For example, an established producer will frequently suggest that, to get the property sold, some changes must be made. There are two variables on this route. The producer may feel that there are some genuine flaws in the piece and that it would benefit from some rewriting. Experience is well worth attending to in many cases. Maybe the pacing is wrong or one of the characters is thinly drawn or the main protagonist is not sympathetic enough—these are legitimate problems. Clearly, it is worth listening intently to this kind of critique—it can make a mediocre script into a good one, a good one into a great one.

The second possibility is that a producer may feel he needs more ammunition to get the piece sold; he may want to "attach" a known writer to the piece who is "network approved." This may not always be acceptable to the original writer, particularly if he or she has labored for months over the first draft, which is, after all, an original idea. It may seem very unfair that someone else, who had nothing to do with the concept's creation, should be thrust into the project and get equal credit, if not more. But you must always keep in mind that the producer wants to get it sold, and this may be the only way. This can be very difficult to call, because sometimes it is unfair and unnecessary, especially if the script is almost perfect and needs only minor adjustments. In those cases, you should politely decline and take your chances as to whether it will go any further. Be careful, though, because if you are a first-time writer, accepting collaboration may be the only way to prevail.

There is a worse eventuality—the producer may want to give the entire script to an experienced writer she knows and leave you with only an "original story created by" credit, for which you have to be paid. But this just doesn't have the charge, the charisma, of the writer or co-writer credit. Again, this varies in acceptability from case to case. As a general rule I would suggest you sleep on it. Give yourself a few days to contemplate whether you are being treated unfairly or whether this is the only truly pragmatic thing to do.

Another possibility in a producer's meeting is that patently absurd and unacceptable changes might be suggested if the producer feels that there is a strong chance of a sale, but only with radical alterations to the script. Your screenplay centers around a black female doctor fighting prejudice in a southern town. They want to change it to a white male doctor who wins the lottery and takes a vacation in the south of France. You scream inside— and then wonder what it would be like to collect fifty thousand dollars as a fee for this ridiculous mutation of your script.

This is a decision no one can make for you. Never do anything you will be ashamed of, but if you would benefit from a nice fat fee and that's that, then take the money and redo your original idea. At least you will have a good roof over your head and enough food protein traveling to the brain to actually continue to write.

Trust your instincts on all of this. Everybody likes to make money, but most of us really care about what our name is attached to. If you just want to create a large bank balance for yourself, then writing or directing commercials would be a better profession to aim for. However, poverty — or having to slave for years at a menial job that takes away much of your creative energy — may not be right for you; it's hard to write fresh, exciting fictional television after a hard day behind the wheel of a cab. It's up to you. On your very first adventure in the business it may be worth your while to take a back seat if that is necessary. It is not a sign of weakness; most producers will respect your humility and won't forget it. Next time they will know you will probably want to move to the front.

If someone in a meeting annoys you, try to keep your temper. Don't be trodden on, ever, but keep your cool. Television professionals have a long memory and charm goes a long way. Be firm and refuse to do anything that is obviously exploitive, but don't scream and shout unless the situation at hand is verging on a horror show. Then you have nothing to lose, as you wouldn't want to work with people like that in any case. There is the same number of creeps and leeches in the television industry as in any other; take care not to get involved with them, but there is no need to be watching out for them at every meeting.

Actually, one of the main rationales for seeking representation is to have someone behind you who knows when to walk, as they say. Make sure you trust that representative, then act as she suggests. No one can write your work for you, but there is no reason why you should know exactly what to do in business matters right from the start. So feel good about delegating that side of the work, at least at the beginning of your career.

You as Prime Mover

I have had a number of agents and lawyers working for me over the last twenty years. Some were good, some were awful—you cannot really know until you put them to the test. One thing I would say with conviction is that no matter how good the person representing you is, you are still the one who has to motivate much of what happens. Sometimes you have to take an aggressive approach to penetrate the system, but you always, without exception, have to be the prime mover. When you have some recognizable successes under your belt, your agent will tend to motivate all kinds of interest, but that can be a few years away. Until then, apart from writing as prolifically as you can, keep up with what is going on in the television business, from network television to home video.

Conclusion

Taking meetings is a late twentieth-century art of the same order as proposal writing. It is not an inspiring skill, but the better you get at it, the more you are able to do justice to your work on the business end. I do not mean you should turn yourself into a slick talker who can handle any situation—the real energy always has to go into the creative writing—but just keep up with what's generally going on; be able to communicate to producers that you are not in an ivory tower but are interested in what television can contain. You can go years without any success in broadcast TV if you are not prepared to see the basic tenets of programming. After all, the very existence of "L.A. Law" and "thirtysomething" does imply that you can write more than just shoot-'em-up crime shows and still make a living on the network level.

Chapter Nine:

Do You
Need
Contacts?

Imagine a technicolor vision of cabals and cadres of closely knit people, tanned and elegant, who are constantly talking to each other on cellular phones, deeply ensconced behind the grey-tinted windows of their white Mercedes sedans, carving up the television business. Newcomers (like you) are sneered at, their manuscripts burned at gilded altars in vast Beverly Hills mansions, where television is never actually watched because this creative elite is far too busy devouring nouvelle cuisine pizza at Spago's or taking warm whirlpool baths by the light of the yellow California moon.

The Paranoia of Elitism

Well, forget it. Yes, quite a few writers, producers and agents mix routinely with studio heads, network chiefs and famous movie stars, living the West Coast good life. But the truth is that the television writing profession is composed of a wide spectrum of working people, all trying to get their work on the air. If you have the talent and the resilience to keep on trying through rejection and maybe even poverty, you can join this group.

Making Contacts

Cultivating contacts has to be considered important, if not always essential. If your writing is sensational—not just very good, but blindingly evocative and commercial at the same time — then maybe you do not need to seek out contacts. Even then, you are going to have to make some effort — calling an agent, finding a producer. Most of us have to use our brain power to find our way in, seeing which people we can get to in order to break through.

It seems to be true that almost everybody knows someone who knows someone who knows someone who is somehow connected with the television business. Given that you are something of an artistic type to begin with, then you can probably think your way through the personal network of your friends, acquaintances and relations to find one person who can help you in some way.

Think about this very carefully. True, you may simply not know anybody, but you would be surprised how far the media have penetrated the body politic, how many people in the last quarter century have moved toward jobs in the entertainment and news gathering sectors. Don't stop the process of trying to find that initial contact until you have thoroughly thought it through. Maybe it was a person you met at a party once who made some helpful offer. Maybe you met someone on a train or a plane. One of your school friends works in television. A second cousin was an extra in an episode of "Highway to Heaven" and had a drink with Michael Landon. Think hard and long about it. The strong likelihood is that if you search your mind and your address book, you can come up with at least a secretary who works for somebody in the business. If you feel that it is not too flimsy a connection — you met for fifteen seconds at a wedding seven years ago — then go for it. Call. Be direct. Ask if that person can help you. Start the chain of telephone calls that can lead to someone with power in television.

If all this fails, you can still follow my earlier guidelines and call an agent by first contacting the Writers' Guild and getting one of their lists. Almost invariably, however, it helps to have some kind of contact.

I do not recommend turning up in New York City or Los Angeles and floating about, trying to get invited to parties and hanging out at the "in" places. It will only usually result in disappointment and debt. That's not to say that it isn't a good idea to be in those two cities if you can without discomfort, but initially the work can be done anywhere, and the phone is a perfect tool to get what you want. The only way to create contacts is to take a deep breath and plunge into calling people about your work.

Networking

Networking is an expression that came into its own in the mid-eighties and means entering a little more scientifically into the business of meeting people and using each other for the betterment of information exchange and career advancement. It sounds crass and exploitive, but in fact it is a valid way of making things happen as long as it amounts to more than a lot of chatting with no results. Wasting time can seem like something else altogether if the atmosphere is sufficiently convivial, but try not to get sucked into a social whirl that gets you nothing except a mini-series of hangovers.

The process may start as humbly as at a writers' get-together in your town. Even though this might involve a group composed of people just casually trying out their hand at a bit of writing, it will usually attract someone else of like mind to you. There is always the chance that if the standard of writing has something to offer, more professionally minded people will join. Then you have ready-made brothers or sisters in arms, ready to tackle the reaching out process together. If you live in or near a large city like Pittsburgh or Grand Rapids or Atlanta, there are always people who have some connections with the media — maybe the local PBS TV outlet or the town newspaper. These may seem less than what you need, but you have to start somewhere, and my experience tells me that, in matters like this, once you actually make the effort to start, there will be progress of an almost organic nature.

Never shrink from asking advice. From anybody or any entity. True, the big Hollywood production companies will probably not help you much unless you know someone — they are too busy or see themselves as too busy. But it is worth your while to take the trouble to contact places that are relevant to your interests and find out where to start.

If you want to write a documentary, you should do some research, find someone or something that has experience in that kind of endeavor, and contact them. With a little bit of enterprise and persistence, you will eventually find someone who will be only too glad to give you some preliminary advice on how to break in or at least who to write to if you have a good idea.

Checking Television Credits

If your goal is to write fiction, find television pieces that you genuinely like and admire and trace who made them. You may not be able to get through to the actual writers, but you will surely find someone who is in some way connected to them.

Your success depends on your degree of determination. It is almost unimaginable that you will fail to make contacts if you keep on trying, not accepting defeat until you have tried every avenue. Let's say you want to do episodic writing. Think of the number of shows that are actually on the air, either in first run or some form of syndication: "Hunter," "Wiseguy," "Miami Vice," "Columbo," "Kojak," "Night Heat," "St. Elsewhere," "Spenser: for Hire," "Cagney and Lacey," "Hill Street Blues," "L.A. Law," "Midnight Caller," "Star Trek—The Next Generation." This is only a partial list of what you will find across the dial. Out of all these shows, there has to be one person who will respond to a phone call or a letter. Check the credits—producer, executive producer, writers, production supervisor, story editor, associate producer, production assistant—if you add up all the possibilities, there are probably thousands of possible contacts. Yes, they are "cold," but they might not all be actually cold people—if they realize that you have admiration for their work and have had the nerve to trace them without being obtrusive or rude, they may take a shine to you and help in some small way over the phone.

Choose some of them and write to them via the production companies involved. It's a long shot, but just by the law of averages, if you try a lot of them, you are likely to find someone who will at the very least return your letter or phone call. Life will present its opportunities to you if you are prepared to put out energy into the unknown. It's a challenge. If you have already written something you consider powerful or competitive, then you have something to talk about. I would not recommend going down any of these roads unless you already have something to show behind all the energetic words of supplication.

There is a contagious quality to good writing. Once you have completed a piece and you are confident that it is worth producing, then you are at the right point to start talking about it. Don't try to network or make a contact until you have work that is as good as you can make it. Just saying you want to write for television, especially to someone in the business, without any proof, is the kiss of death. Professionals cannot take the dream writer seriously, because it is very annoying to hear someone say that they aspire to something that is your life's work. It's like telling a great tennis player that you think you could easily knock that soft little ball over the net and be great at it—but you have never actually played the game. It's insulting.

The rules are really your own. Set your goal and trace logical paths to reach it. My guidelines are based on the journeys of many people, but if I have to examine my own, then I see there are individual, personal routes that no one else has taken. The answer to the question of how best to go about it is a combination of personal hunches and other people's experience. It just isn't like deciding to become a mechanical engineer or a lawyer—this is a convoluted path.

Working in Production

Another way to break in is to get involved in production. I know of several writers who gradually realized that they could write after being part of a production team. Just seeing the script gradually turn into a televised piece is stimulating, and sometimes assistant producers or even production assistants feel that they are capable of pulling something off. They see what it takes to make something viable for the screen; they get to know writers and directors; they go home after a day's work and start putting words down on paper. By this time they probably know at least a few influential professionals, and it is easy to get to such people if you have done a good, conscientious job on the set or in the editing room.

Surprisingly, you can gain a fair amount of credibility even if you have only been getting the coffee. As long as you have ingratiated yourself with good, solid work that has obviously contributed to getting the show produced, it is a very real first step. You could even employ some cunning and pay your dues on the production end, all the while waiting for your moment to present some good writing to someone you have actually worked for. And even if your working colleague fails to take the bait, you still have an ideal opportunity to ask about who might be interested in your script or idea. I am not suggesting you do a half-hearted job in production while biding your time, waiting for writing glory. If a member of the staff is not truly pulling her weight, it gets noticed. But there's a middle ground where you can use what you have learned and who you have met to get you into the writing fraternity. I can't tell you the number of times someone on my team has told me in a low-key way that he has a screenplay or a great idea for a documentary or even a new game show idea.

Generally speaking, those who have already worked in some capacity in television have a fairly accurate idea of what it would take to actually create something worthwhile. But not always. Occasionally I have had to listen to ridiculous, half-baked ideas even from folks who have been through the process. There is no guarantee that a person who has helped put something as complex as a television production together can project into what it really takes to write something. The advantage is there if you can write.

Be Cautious About Who You Talk To

Talking to people about your ideas can be a hair-raising experience. One of the worst problems that comes up is that you will tell someone enthusiastically about a concept or a fully written script and the response will be: "Oh, you know, that's very bizarre ... that's exactly like something that I've been thinking about— in fact, I'm working on it right now...." This can be true, of course, but more often than not it is chronic delusion, or worse, a disingenuous lie. This is one of the most daunting aspects of sharing your visions, particularly within a very competitive sub-culture that is only partially in pursuit of art. However, I maintain that many workers in television still retain enough idealism and sense of camaraderie that in most cases you will receive positive, real help from your colleagues. You just have to be careful about who you talk to. Avoid people who say they are doing exactly the same work, because you may find your own bright ideas in someone else's proposal or treatment very quickly. You can usually tell, though, if that is the case. Be cautious rather than suspicious.

The main reason to do premarketing networking is simply to get useful feedback on the basic quality of your writing. In the case of screenplays or treatments, it is almost essential to get the benefit of others' opinions before you move into pitching. Even the unversed (in television skills) can be important critics. True, most people do not know how to read a screenplay, but they can usually do very well with a treatment or outline. You may be able to avoid some very embarrassing omissions or faux pas if you get a friend to read your work. Relatives are not generally useful as early readers because they tend to love your writing no matter what its quality, so concentrate on trusted friends and press them to be as honest as they can.

It is amazing how someone who has no involvement whatsoever in show business can sometimes track mistakes in consistency or even something more subtle like pacing or characterization. This process of amateur criticism is not really networking, but it is a necessary prerequisite.

Get all the bugs out before you decide to go truly public—you simply don't need these kinds of critiques when your major concern is selling. After all, even after you have polished the piece or the proposal to the best of your ability, including the use of friends' wisdom, you are still going to encounter criticism and possibly rejection, so make sure you are putting your best foot forward when you meet agents, producers, readers, story editors, programmers or financial backers. Their modifications should be on the high critical level based upon experience and the need to be commercial—your friends' changes will probably be far more fundamental; and it almost goes without saying that you should do your utmost to give the professionals only the more subtle critical tasks.

TV as Teamwork

Television is the most collaborative of the media arts, even writing. Sometimes there is actually a co-writer on your project, either by your own design or imposed by the producers. Beyond that, the actual production of a film can involve over a hundred people, counting everyone from agents to the publicists and promotional departments of studios or production companies. But collaboration starts even before all that—in the feedback matrix you might want to set up and in the number of people who you will pitch to before you get a sale.

At times this can be a little overwhelming. The writing game would seem to be a solitary one, where you trade off security and being bored or oppressed in some office for the lonely but liberated task of the creator. The truth is that in the context of the late twentieth-century media, you are not alone except in the essential act of creation. After you have written the script or the proposal, you are caught in a web of many people, and unless you are lucky enough to have an agent or partner who will take care of everything for you across the board, you have to accept this. The aim is to be with the right people at the right juncture in the gestation of your work.

Chapter Ten:

CONFIDENCE

CONFIDENCE, YOU WOULD THINK, COMES WITH SUCCESS. THE truth is that even after it comes, many creative artists find it difficult to sustain. How many times have we read or had first-hand knowledge of an artist who seems very much on the rise yet complains of chronic insecurity and self-doubt? Obviously the feeling of uncertainty is even more extreme when there has been little or no success.

Does Success Bring Confidence?

Even great and renowned artists have fits of doubt—not all of them, but certainly most. Bob Dylan had disturbingly dry periods. So did Tennessee Williams, F. Scott Fitzgerald, and Stanley Kubrick—probably even Shakespeare had off days. It's a natural part of creativity. Couple doubt with the modern pressure caused by pitching and selling your work in a hotly contested marketplace and you have a universally experienced problem.

How is this intangible quality—half visceral, half rational—to be nurtured and sustained? The only real answer to the question of how to maintain confidence is through practice and daily attention.

Renewing Your Confidence Daily

The best way to keep your confidence going while in the process of trying to make a success of your TV writing career is by maintaining, as best you can, an objective attitude about the actual quality of your work, not allowing any periods of stasis or even stagnation to unnerve you unduly.

Talking to trusted friends about your writing and showing it to them whenever it feels right are two ways to preserve a certain equanimity about your creativity. On the sales side, keep in touch with the medium as much as you can, constantly looking out for appropriate places where there might be real receptivity to your particular kind of writing. Read *Variety*, *Entertainment Weekly*, *Hollywood Reporter*, *Electronic Media*, *Backstage*, the Arts and Leisure section of the *New York Times*, or your equivalent local newspaper, *Rolling Stone*, *Millimeter*, and even *TV Guide*.

Though the general public reads most of these publications, it is surprising how much real information they constantly purvey about what's going on in show business and what the TV networks and syndicators are currently entranced with. Confidence as to where you fit in and where you might fit in the near future is created and re-created just by knowing that you are aware of the flow and are remaining thoroughly conscious of what's actually going on here and now in a totally commercialized field.

Learning to Maintain "Attack"

Let's go deeper into the question of basic confidence. In the creative writing area, much of what we deem to be confidence is brought about by your ability to maintain "attack." What is "attack"? The best way to define it is to demonstrate its manifestation in other artistic arenas. The way Eric Clapton launches into a blues guitar riff is "attack." The deftness of a Picasso brushstroke, no matter how minimal, is another example. The way Robert de Niro speaks a line; the comedic aptness of a Woody Allen-directed scene — these are all "attacks" of the best kind. They show a fine synthesis of experience and immediate consciousness coupled with the exacting nuances of their artistic skill — all of this combined makes for a refined hold upon an art form.

As a writer, I find that the way to cultivate this grasp and execution is to write as often as possible. Even if you are having enormous difficulty in getting the right thing down on paper, just go ahead and write something. It is astonishing how successful you can be when you throw caution to the wind and just get into the act of writing — even if you think you are bound to be creating gibberish because of your so-called state of mind, your writer's block, because your wife argued with you, your dog went on the carpet, and so on ad nauseam. The act of attacking the piece of paper, even with an angry abandon, can often result in amazingly good writing — in good "attack."

A similar situation can be pulled off in the ancillary area of getting your work seen and sold. If you can't get an agent, then just make cold calls. Designate a day or two to making lists of worthwhile people and organizations to contact and then simply make the calls. If you already have an agent but she doesn't seem to be doing anything to advance your career, then get on the phone and push her a bit. Act with strength but not irrationality. Maybe there has not been enough time to get round to your work yet, so be careful; but if you have already taken that into account and there still seems to be nothing going on, then act for yourself. Manufacture confidence by creating your own momentum. Action is the key word here.

Getting Organized

Priming and psyching yourself to learn how to both write and sell correctly can often seem to be insuperable tasks. Just like any other area of endeavor, you must get to it step by step. You may find it progressive and kind of comforting to make lists and simple flow diagrams, for your own eyes only. What do you really want to write? How long will it take? Who is likely to be able to give you an objective opinion as to whether it's any good or not? Where should it go? Who are the agents to contact? What should you say in the cover letter? How should you characterize yourself? How many hours a day do you need to work (and for how many days) on all these components of the progress toward eventual success? Maybe this is too big a list to start with, but each of these elements can have its own minilist. You have to get organized. Putting the situation in order on paper is an effective antidote to depression, sloth, and wanting to forget the whole aspiration and go back to being an office worker with a regular paycheck at the end of the week.

It is also vital to perceive clearly all the necessary steps to get your work to the buyer. This may also have to be written out in flow chart form.

In order to embark successfully upon a career that demands great willpower and an ability to renew confidence on a daily basis, you must have a realistic view of just what writing for television is all about. The public, the viewer, is the bottom line in terms of ultimate acceptance. But between the public and you lies the apparatus of the industry. That complex, entrenched infrastructure is what you have to penetrate. At the beginning the only way not to be overwhelmed by its size and visible power is to first break it down into the fields that interest you and then further reduce those alternatives until you know exactly where you want to be.

At that point you will find that it is generally a matter of intensive focusing and contacting the right people. You must be superrealistic and aim at people who will respond, like agents and producers, rather than network programming heads or the high powered, semicelebrity executives of the most successful supplier production companies.

Put Yourself at Ease

Next you must go inside yourself — don't worry about what anyone else does — and decide in what ways you inspire confidence in yourself and bring out the best in yourself, particularly as you will soon have to interface with people you do not know and have never met. Do whatever you have to do within reason to get it on. If you have to make a crucial telephone call — to an agent, a lawyer, a secretary at a production company, whoever — make sure you don't allow any other alien or negative thoughts to get in the way. Clear the way for yourself. Avoid environments where other people are talking, playing music or watching television. Make your immediate work space your office, even if it's only for the ten minutes of the next phone call. Don't make calls too early in the morning, both for your sake and for the sake of the recipient. No one wants to get cold calls at five after nine in the morning, unless there is an obvious and unavoidable urgency.

Be alert. Get protein to the brain—eat. Don't make sleepy phone calls; get a good night's sleep before the big meeting. Don't worry too much about your style of dress for a meeting, but make sure your clothes are clean and unwrinkled. If you are Norman Mailer or David Mamet, this may not matter in the least, but if people don't know you, try not to load the dice against yourself by ignoring these little details. When you are at the beginning of your writing career, it's all part of the pitch.

Love Your Work

One of the most crucial aspects of retaining confidence and energy is remaining realistic about where you stand and how to narrow your aspirations without dropping the dream. The dream is not only that you will write a lauded prime-time movie-of-the-week or initiate a wonderful new situation comedy that nudges "The Cosby Show" and "Roseanne" out of the top spots. It is that you will create something that conforms to your vision of your project, with the show that is finally broadcast resembling at least in spirit the first ideas that were scooting round your cerebrum.

If you write something that you love, it should not be that important whether it gets developed or produced. The first determinant of success has to be your own feeling about your work. Nobody can replace that very special, private thrill.

Now, if no one else likes it in the least, then take another look at your own objectivity and decide whether everyone else is crazy and you're the only clear-headed person around. Next, the reaction of those you are trying to sell to is a big consideration.

The whole point of being a television writer is to get your work on the tube, so you cannot rest on your laurels for too long. It is important, however, to evaluate your work without the constant impact of buyer reaction tainting your opinion. Just show the piece, whatever it is, to someone whose taste you respect and find out what he thinks; press for complete honesty. It is vital that your friends or relatives not stroke you too much—you need to get some sane, balanced take on how good your stuff really is. If you get this honest appraisal and it is positive, yet the showbiz types reject your piece, then you are the only one who can decide how good it really is. If you genuinely love what you've made, then even if you get a hundred rejections, you should still not let your confidence suffer. You've achieved something that you admire, and that's great. Let no one take that away from you. After all, many of the greatest artworks were initially rejected, even reviled. You cannot get too hung up on what other people say.

Are You Barking Up the Right Tree?

The typical writer needs as much support as she can get without becoming silly or self-deluded. Feedback from a nearly impenetrable industry is not necessarily a decent evaluation of the quality of a work. The factors of timing and topicality are central to this kind of professional writing. To succeed in this game, you have to adopt two simultaneous self-critical attitudes. First, find out how good you are the best way you can. Second, compare your suitability/appropriateness/timing sense to commercial television reality. Think about these two mental processes and then make your decision about the wisdom of choosing this as a profession. Until you actually make a sale, which could take a while even after you have completed and corrected the script or proposal, it's difficult to judge your own skills and talent. After a sale it is obviously easier to see whether you are going to make a life of it.

Every time you think you are barking up the wrong tree and that "nobody in the business will ever take me seriously," step back a bit and decide whether you are just whining because you aren't living the dream at your pace, without taking into consideration the rigors of the industry. If no company buys anything for ten years, you will have to be a little brutal with yourself about whether you have anything to offer or, less negatively, whether the TV industry is the right place for your specific brand of creativity. But don't be discouraged if you have little success for a few years, as nasty as it may be to live through such a bleak interval. Press on, make money any way you can, and wait for that time when somebody in TV sees how great your work is.

Chapter Eleven:

A NEW
NETWORK
WRITER

ONE OF THE BEST WAYS TO ILLUSTRATE THE PROCESS AND
examine the minutiae of getting a script sold and produced is to
inquire into the details of an actual deal with a real, live person
who pulled it off. I chose Ronni Simon, who sold a script to
ABC and that achieved ratings success and propelled her into a
professional television writing career. The value of investigating
her particular path to success is that she was a relative neophyte,
and her example is neither too exalted nor too idiosyncratic.

A New Scriptwriter Succeeds

Ronni was a writer who had never dealt with television executives. Married to a successful photographer, living on Martha's
Vineyard, her life was fine without diving into the competitive,
stressful world of network television. However, at some point she
got the bug and decided she wanted to get her work on television.
It was a long haul, though not too long, and eventually she tasted
the fruits of success and fulfillment in the field. It would be mis-
leading to say that Ronni had a driving ambition to write network
movies-of-the-week from the time she was a young girl — the truth
is that she started to write a column for a local newspaper, developed a taste for the sweetness of writing humorous pieces, began
to feel that she had what it took to move on to bigger things, and

made moves in that direction over a period of a few years.

Now, Ronni was fortunate to know some influential people, but it still was a path she went down that represented the best that she could do. It should prove educational and even inspirational because it demonstrates a dogged pursuit of a goal and the way things really happen.

The character traits she displays and the way she nurtured her determination and concentration are very useful as a paradigm of how to succeed in this business. Also, the details she reveals on how to act before you get approval should be useful to any writer. All in all her experiences should be instructive to anyone who wants to get into the field. That is why I interviewed her in the summer of 1989 in her house on Martha's Vineyard.

Beginnings

DAVID SILVER: What was the name of the television film you wrote, and give me the basic stuff.

RONNI SIMON: The movie was called *Addicted to His Love* and it was for the ABC network. It was a two-hour movie-of-the-week starring Barry Bostwick and Polly Bergen, and it was shown on the network in the 1988 season.

DS: What was the earliest germ of this work?

RS: In this case, the producers had a commitment from ABC. They had already sold the movie, and they were just looking for a writer. They had sold it. They simply had to convince ABC that the story was solid and there was an acceptable writer.

DS: For the sake of my readers, let's go back to the beginning of your writing career.

RS: I actually have a great story. I was working on an independent film, on the production side, doing continuity — clapboards and that kind of thing. I had been wondering what to do with myself — I used to be a potter, so I was thinking, What's next? On this first film job I wasn't getting paid, just expenses. It was in Ocean City, New Jersey. I read the script of the film — the writer had gotten an AFI [American Film Institute] grant. I was inspired to think that I could do it too. There were two children on the set who were actors in the movie and one had a real stage mother. This little girl had dyed her hair. The whole thing gave me an idea for a sitcom about a child star with the stage mother and the whole bit, and I called it "Casey's Mom."

I thought, Who do I know who could help me? and the person that came to mind was Garson Kanin, not because I'm that friendly with him but I know him from Martha's Vineyard. He was real friendly and nice; he just seemed the kind of person that might help.

So I made a copy of "Casey's Mom" and I sent a letter to him saying what you'd expect. "Dear Garson . . . enclosed is this treatment . . . I understand perfectly if you are too busy . . . just pretend you never got it . . ." I gave him every out in the world. Disregard it, rip it up, I'll never mention it, you never heard from me, next time I see you we'll ignore the whole thing. I mean it was kind of funny, but I was basically serious, saying that this was pretty outrageous of me sending it to him, and I understood, whatever his reaction.

I must have sent it out on a Monday, and I didn't even Federal Express it, but on the Wednesday I got a call from him and he was very theatrical, like "Ronni, darling, this is Garson . . . I got your treatment and it just looks fine to me, but quite frankly I don't know anything about television sitcoms. With your permission, I'm photocopying copies, and I'm sending one to Norman Lear and one to Lorimar." Obviously, I said, "Go ahead. That's really sweet of you." He sent me a letter listing who he had sent it to, and I got a call really quickly from Brigitte Potter at Lorimar. She said, "I'd really like to meet with you. Garson just wrote such a dear note about you and next time you're in New York. . . ."

Cut to New York . . . well, there were problems with it. The networks used to have a problem with shows about show business—though there were some exceptions—it was like some sort of unwritten rule. So it didn't go much further. The feeling was that people in the Midwest wouldn't be able to relate to a child star. They've changed now, but that was that.

Someone with a track record could have made them break
the rules, but not someone breaking in. Everybody's looking
for an excuse not to read your material, not to like it, to dismiss
it, so you just can't give them any of those excuses. They did
ask me if I had any other ideas. I did. This helped me get an
agent.

DS: I know you started writing for the *Vineyard Gazette*, then the
film gig. What was the timespan from then to getting to the
point we're now talking about?

RS: Just a few months from when I was on the film in the winter.
This stuff was probably in the spring. I had a good sample of
my writing. But then, basically, reality set in. They said, you
know, it's very rare for somebody to just break right in.

DS: How hard is it to break into sitcoms?

RS: I would say that sitcoms are the hardest form. If you want
to start writing for television, this is probably not the way.

DS: So you're at the point where they've more or less rejected
your work.

RS: Okay, so then I decided I did want to move out to L.A.

DS: So people implied that if you would commit yourself to L.A.,
you would get in?

RS: Well, maybe not quite like that, but I wanted to move there
and see what I could do. In the interim I had gotten an idea
for a feature-length movie called *Private Property*, and I decided
that I would go home and work on that. I wrote that with
Richard Lourie who has since gone on to writing well-
recognized books. I didn't have an agent at this point.

I did read a book about writing called *Screenplay* by Syd
Field. It told me exactly how to write a screenplay and then
we did it, made all the copies, registered it at the Writers'
Guild, and then sent it to producers and agents — you know,
just sent it, sent it, sent it, sent it and basically got lots of
rejections. But one person read it who thought it was pretty
off the wall — but it was funny, it really was. That person, Peter
Grunwald, was interested in me as a writer. He worked for
Charles Evans, the producer.

DS: What did you learn from this period?

RS: The most important thing is perseverance. I had so many rejections, I could have given up at every turn. Either you have a driving force that makes you do it or you don't. I think it will pay off, but there are no guarantees. If you do have the drive, there's something telling you that there's a reason to write.

Anyway, Peter Grunwald was someone I didn't know—he was a friend of a friend of a friend. That's another thing I would say: You just have to be very aggressive in contacting friends, people. Everyone knows somebody who knows somebody.

Your Script as a Valuable Writing Example

RS: Everybody has to write a spec script—a script for free—and you don't usually sell that script, but it's your calling card. You need that just to get your foot in the door so that somebody will meet with you and then you can wow them. Next, you have to get yourself in a position for someone to help you. Charles Evans had been the executive producer of *Tootsie*. He was the money person, with not that much creative input. His brother is Bob Evans, the producer. I kept working on *Private Property*, doing this take on it, that take on it—so many different things—and nothing worked. Six months of total frustration.

Then what happened? Oh yes . . . I went to see a foreign film called *Le Beau Mariage*. Sitting there, it gave me an idea for a movie, completely unlike *Private Property*. I took an element of *Le Beau Mariage* and *Palm Beach Story*, the old Preston Sturges film, and I came up with a whole other movie that ended up being called *Marry Me*.

I wrote a ten-page treatment and gave it to Peter. He said, "This is great. This is it. I think Charles will go for it." It was a cute, fresh, romantic comedy idea. Charles Evans read it and really liked it. Before I knew it I had my first development deal to write a movie. This meant that I had been hired to write a movie for this producer.

Once I was hired by a producer who's a signatory to the Writers' Guild, I was invited to join the Guild, and there's lots of benefits. You're considered a professional, because you can't get in the Writers' Guild unless you've been hired to write something by an accredited producer. I didn't have to join it but I did. It's like a Catch-22. You can't get in it until you've been hired to write something, and you can't write things unless you're in it. But there's this little window where you can get your first deal. Once you're in the Guild, you don't have to beg. People know you've already sold things. It's the next rung of the ladder.

DS: What happened next?

RS: I wrote *Marry Me* and worked for Charles and Peter. Finished it. It was cute but it had some problems and didn't get made.

DS: So what did you do?

RS: I had a script. A script can sit on a shelf for five, six, ten years and then all of a sudden . . . nothing had come of it so far, but I had a concrete thing to shop around to get an agent. So I approached somebody at William Morris and Victoria Wisdom at APA—Agency for the Performing Arts. Also, I asked friends if they knew any agents.

Victoria loved the script and really wanted to represent me with APA. They were considered one of the top five agencies and had an office in New York City, which was important to me. She seemed great, so I pretty much committed to her.

Victoria helped me in a big way. She put me together with a writer—Susan Nanus. Barbra Streisand's production company, Barwood Productions, was very interested in my idea if it could be a comedy for Barbra to star in and direct.

So Susan and I got together, and after working for just two hours we came up with a great story. We made a little outline, and I guess Barbra Streisand liked it enough to give it the go-ahead. We then wrote something called *American Harvest*, which was a comedy. At that time, Barbra decided she didn't want to do comedies any more. She wanted to do *Nuts*. Most people really liked it, but nothing came of our piece. The great thing was that Susan and I formed a partnership and wrote three movies together, one for Paramount and one for Tri-Star.

Then I moved to Martha's Vineyard. I was a new mother

and had my son, Willie, who was about nine months old. Susan got a deal for a television movie, so we started to do things seperately. I was not being as aggressive about my career because of Willie. I did write one movie when he was six months old.

"The Break"

RS: Anyway, then I moved to William Morris. They said there was a producer who was looking for a writer for a TV movie. We talked a little about the idea. The original title was *Sisterhood* and the idea that she told me was this: Four women band together to get back at a man who took advantage of them, a con man.

DS: Was it a true story?

RS: Yes. It's based on a real story. It took place in a small town in northern California. He was this balding, paunchy guy. I'd read about him in *People* magazine. There was a media blitz about him.

DS: How did they characterize him?

RS: He was a bigamist. A woman, Danielle Alexander, bought the rights to the women's story for about ten grand. This guy married one, almost married another one. He took their credit cards. He was convicted for bigamy and larceny. The producers liked the written concept of a con man and the women who get back at him. So they sent me all the press releases and news stories so I could start thinking about it. They said, "Go wild with the idea, just take off."

DS: They wanted you to write and do research?

RS: Yeah. You have to come up with the whole story. They gave me basically a one-line idea, which is very typical when you meet with producers. I had a conference call with them.

I talked about my ideas a little bit, and they said, "Oh great, great. How about this?" They all have their ideas that they think are brilliant. So you take it all in and say, "Yeah, that sounds good . . . sure . . . yeah." And from there it all flowed rather quickly. Before I knew it I had a deal. It was one of the easiest things. It literally fell out of the sky.

A Network Meeting

DS: Any obstacles you noticed?

RS: One obstacle is that you have to be network approved. The networks actually have a list of approved writers. I wasn't on the list, obviously, but they approved me after seeing some of my work. That was the first hurdle. I was temporarily approved. My agent started working on the deal, and I was told I should go out to L.A. to meet with the producers. I guess I was naive or something—I still didn't think it was all definite. By then I'd written a seven-act outline with all the scenes numbered, so I went out to L.A. and met with ABC.

The meeting was with the four independent producers, Scott Spiegel, who was the executive at ABC assigned to our movie, and Ted Hambert, head of ABC Movie-of-the-Week—the producers were very impressed that he was in on the meeting. It was funny. He didn't even have a copy of the treatment and had no idea what it was about. It was hard because then we had to pitch it to him as if he knew nothing.

Normally in these situations everybody has read the treatment, but because Ted knew absolutely nothing about it, we had to go from point A, pretty much scene by scene. These guys are used to maybe half-hour meetings, but we were into this meeting about an hour and a half already and were only up to act five. Then Ted said he had to go but that it sounded great, and if we could pull it off that would be terrific. "Okay, see you later." He and Scott walked out and we just looked at each other. Not having any experience, I thought, "God, he thought we were idiots," but when they talked to him later, he had given the go-ahead.

From Script to Production

RS: So I went back East and wrote the script. I had all my blueprints. I finished it in a few months, got the first draft to L.A., and they loved it. They said it was the best first draft they'd ever got. They had some comments and sent me some changes, which I made. They also asked me to make the changes in a hurry because the networks were planning the next season, and it's all a matter of timing. If we had missed by a week, we would have had to wait months, and by then they may not have been so excited about it; there may have been a new hot movie or whatever. We had to get it to them the week before Thanksgiving. So I hurried. It took me five days. I sent it, and got a call from ABC just two or three days later saying they had received the go-ahead.

ABC considered it a first draft, and I was told that it was the first time ABC had given the go-ahead on a first draft.

By the beginning of December, they were in pre-production. I went out there two weeks before Christmas to meet with the producers and go over the final draft. There were two drafts and three polishes, I think, and you don't get paid until you've done them all. After I met with the director they had hired I went back home and they started.

This is my experience with television and it's not that unusual. I met the producer in May 1987 and was officially hired by June 1987. I wrote the script in September, finished it in November. The show was in production by December and on the air in March 1988. So in less than a year I had made my deal, written the script, and it was on the air. That's fascinating to me. You could never do that with a feature film. With features, you are lucky if it takes only two years from when you're hired to write something to get your piece in the theater. It's more likely to be shelved for years.

From Idea to Execution

DS: If you had an original idea, not an assigned one, what would be the very first steps you would take?

RS: Get an agent first. Producers will not read [unsolicited] material because they are afraid of getting sued.

DS: Will agents read unsolicited material?

RS: Yes, because that's their job.

DS: All agents?

RS: Yeah. Agents at William Morris still start out in the mail room. A beginning agent might be the one to read it or an assistant.

DS: If you were living in Shreveport or Quebec or upstate New York somewhere, how would you go about finding an agent?

RS: I would contact the Writers' Guild, either East or West, and request a list of agents. They have a complete list, and there are lots and lots of agents.

DS: Is there any way to infer from that list who has agented what?

RS: Yes. You can write the agency and ask for a client list. They'll send it to you.

DS: So you find an agent. How would you suggest actually talking to that agent?

RS: Well, your work is going to speak for itself. I mean, you have to write a great script; there's no way of getting round it. You can't sell an agent an idea. Also, you have to be charming and nice and pleasant and fun; put on your best face. But you have to have written something really great, and obviously you have to write an intelligent cover letter. Also, when you write a spec script, it has to look like a professional script.

DS: Would you recommend watching TV movies?

RS: Definitely.

DS: How about feature scripts?

RS: Why not? Sure. For TV, think about true stories, issue-oriented stuff — though those are usually assigned. Think about family dramas, etc.

DS: To sum up a bit: What are the bottom line things that you must accept with humility as a first-time writer?

RS: You can't be arrogant about anything. You're not in the driver's seat as the writer, and you never are until you become a producer. Writers do not have clout unless they are Neil Simon or Woody Allen; there are just a handful. The reality is that they love you and need you in the beginning. As soon as they have the script, it's like, "Who are you? What's your name?"

DS: Anything you would do differently now?

RS: Well, if I'd wanted to continue with my television-writing career, given that the TV movie was really a success, I would have moved to Los Angeles. I think you have to live in L.A. to write for television. You can write that first script anywhere, but people shouldn't think that they can continue a TV career while manning a little hardware store in Wisconsin. If you get your break, you move out there to remain successful.

DS: But you wouldn't suggest moving out there in order to get your first break?

RS: I don't think you have to, and it could be very frustrating just washing cars if you don't get your break.

DS: Major agents are in New York City and Los Angeles. Eventually you have to put together the air fare, hotels, to visit them, right?

RS: It's really hard work. A big phrase in Hollywood is "execution." Everybody has ideas. If you get into a cab there and tell the driver you're a writer, he'll say, "Oh, I want to be a writer. What do you think of this . . . ?" But can you pull it off? Can you write 120 pages — characters, plot, dialogue? It's hard.

Footnotes to a Successful Beginning

Ronni started on the road to television writing by contacting Garson Kanin, who is a major writer by anybody's standards. But what if you don't have those kind of connections? You might think that Ronni's is an unusual case. Clearly, she did receive some impetus from this connection. But as she says, she wasn't a close friend of Kanin's, and she did take the initial step of sending him a letter with a copy of her sitcom treatment. Significantly, this didn't really go anywhere — it took several more links of the chain to get to Charles Evans and the eventual offer of the movie-of-the-week assignment.

You have to work out your own path to success and choose a way to start on it. I don't think it's too farfetched to say that *everyone* has some friend of a friend of a friend who can help in some way, even if only with advice. Maybe your search will take a little longer than did Ronni Simon's, who happens to live on Martha's Vineyard, traditionally a colony for writers of all kinds. But with some concentration and dedication, there is no reason, if you have the writing talent to begin with, why you can't invent a starter modus operandi of your own to get your stuff seen.

What emerges from my interview with Ronni is that there is no given route to TV writing success. The crucial thing is to put yourself in the running. That means fighting to find the right people to listen to you and look at your work. Once the process of osmosis has fixed you in the mind's of influential people, something is bound to happen sooner or later. Then you must be ready to go down whatever road opens up to you.

Although Ronni originally wanted to do sitcoms, she kept writing and eventually found success in a related genre — the comedy TV feature. She got into the business by following her heart on the matter — she wanted to write for TV and, by a circuitous route that could not possibly have been predicted, reached her goal, had a ratings success, earned some decent money, and put herself in the race for further success in the industry.

Chapter Twelve:
WRITING DRAMA FOR PUBLIC TV

THE LAST CHAPTER GAVE US SOME INSIGHTS INTO WRITING FOR network television and also showed some real situations that writers find themselves in. The next three chapters offer an inside look at the receptivity factors of pay cable TV, corporate sponsors and public television. How do high-level decision makers and advisors to bigger decision makers feel about the material coming in to them?

Executive Intelligence

I want to start with public television, where many good quality writers get their work developed and produced. More significantly for the purposes of this book, public television is where a lot of new writers would like to be. Is public TV more receptive to high-class work? What kind of drama are they looking for? What are the processes by which you get your work to the right people and get it financed? To find the answers to these questions, I talked to Lynne Doherty, Manager of Program Development for the highly esteemed "American Playhouse" series, at her office in New York City.

I started the conversation by asking her about her specialties and her education, so that you could get a closer look at the sort of professional you will be dealing with if working in public television is your goal. Lynne is extremely sharp and knowledgeable, and she's typical of fiction decision makers working for public and pay cable television. Also, I wanted to glean from her the exact process of elimination your writing goes through before it reaches her desk. Her answers will give you a better idea of what treatment you are likely to get if you submit to an organization like "American Playhouse."

Lynne's Background

DAVID SILVER: How long have you been doing this?

LYNNE DOHERTY: I started here just under three years ago, in September 1986. I was originally hired to be the assistant to the director of program development, Miranda Barry. Miranda departed to pursue her own writing career. So now I'm doing this.

DS: What were you doing before this?

LD: A bit of freelance production work. I was only a year out of college. I was still pretty green.

DS: But that's interesting in itself. Assuming you're going to be modest and not say you're just wonderful and brilliant, how did you come to make this step so quickly into a fairly powerful position?

LD: I think it was a combination of good fortune and good timing, as it turns out to be in many jobs. Plus it was a kind of meshing of sensibilities. I can't think of too many other producing organizations that would actually suit my sensibilities as well as "Playhouse" has proven to. I think there is that kind of sympatico that developed between us here.

DS: Were you a writer at all?

LD: No, I come from a very theoretical background. I have a degree in Semiotics, which is a branch of literary theory based in psychoanalytic theory and Marxist theory — at least the particular framework that I was in. It also was applied widely to film and other kinds of popular culture, so I'd done a lot of critical and academic writing and a lot of analyzing of films and other texts. It was pretty solidly theoretical. Most people at Brown used the Semiotics department as a film major and really went into making films; the degree was something that they took begrudgingly. I loved the theory and academic side of it, but I didn't go anywhere near production till I'd been out of school for a few months and was drawn into it sort of unwittingly. It had always been the literary side that had appealed to me. After about a year of production I realized that, for me with my background and my interests, if I was to have some kind of influence it would be in the pre-production stage. I came from a strong literary background and had a pretty good understanding of the working of text.

Through the Eyes of the Script Reader

DS: When you first started this, was it hard to get into the business of judging people's work?

LD: My first impulse was to read everything that came into the office. We usually get thirty to forty scripts a week, and because I'd never been exposed to that broad a range of work, that was how I got myself acclimated as quickly as I could. I burned out very quickly and eventually had to stop because you soon get to the point where, if you're trying to absorb that much, you begin to hate everything you read. Whether it was addressed to me or anybody in the office, I read it. I did get to know the best and worst ends of the spectrum. I was also able to refine my own taste and sensibility and get a better handle on what kind of material I respond to strongly.

DS: How many scripts can you read in a week and still maintain your critical acumen?

LD: When we're at the height of our script submission season, I can actually get through ten or fifteen in a week. If I'm spending a day at home all I do is read scripts, not taking phone calls, not doing correspondence. Some scripts you get halfway through and you know that it's not going to be something you want to pursue.

DS: Give me a breakdown of where most of the scripts come from and how they get to you.

LD: We get the full range. We're one of the few places that will accept unsolicited submissions. By "unsolicited" most organizations mean unagented scripts or scripts that don't have a producer or a director attached to them, but oftentimes an unproduced or unpublished writer sends the work. So it probably breaks down into pretty even thirds. About a third comes from writers themselves, some of whom are established, some not. Another third comes from agents, who sometimes are sending you a script they specifically want you to produce. I think their hope is always that you will produce it, but if not that, then it's a way of acquainting you with the work of one of their clients. A very important part of what any script development office does, besides justifying those eighteen shows that are going to go on the air next season or the season after, is staying in touch as well as we can with the whole range of writers out there.

What the unsolicited submissions allow us to do is to accept scripts from young, unknown, unproduced writers — spotting talent early. And I may get a script from a young writer that isn't ready for production or may not be right for us for one reason or another; but this writer is someone I can encourage to send more work and five or six years down the line you see him or her starting to gain an audience and get things produced.

DS: And the last third?

LD: That third, I would say, would be producers and directors, some of whom are known, people who we know or may have worked with before, and some who are producers just out of USC Film School, trying to get their first project off the ground. So within each of these three categories there's a broad range of people who are sending stuff to us.

DS: Let's just talk about the real neophytes. Let's just say, over a long period of time, you get one hundred scripts from people who've never been produced, don't have an agent, are not represented — out of a hundred, how many are good, first of all, and second, how many would you produce?

LD: It's going to be an ugly statistic. I would say eighty, eighty-five out of a hundred are scripts that don't need to be taken another step further after your initial read.

DS: But can you detect out of that 85 percent which ones you might want to give a phone call to or write a letter to? You see there's something of a spark there. What do you do when you see that spark?

LD: Just what you said. I would either make a call so that I can personally let the person know that, while this isn't something we can pursue, I would like to see more of their work in the future, or if there's one specific thing I think they could work on, I'd let them know that.

I tend not to give lengthy critiques, probably because I need to save my energies for the scripts that we're actually planning to produce. My tendency when I first began this job was to want to give everyone a detailed critique of their work, but I finally realized that, first of all, it's not really my job, and second, they haven't asked me for that. It's almost presumptuous to do that unless someone has asked you to. But generally if there's one clear problem, with one strong adjustment that could improve it greatly, I'll point out that one thing.

DS: But you won't give a dissertation on it.

LD: No. Truthfully, I don't have time to even call all the writers, but I'll tend to give a more thoughtful written response. Most of the stuff we get is at least intelligible. There are more unfortunate pieces where, five pages in, you still haven't seen an English sentence yet. But most of what we get at least makes sense, and people show some understanding of stage play or screenplay or teleplay form, depending on what genre they're working in. What I find most lacking in a lot of the scripts I read—and this doesn't just go for the unsolicited scripts; it's true of a lot of the agented scripts as well—is some sense of a connection to the world at large. I think with young writers you tend to get a lot of personal stories, which is fine, but I find myself asking young writers to ask themselves, would they find their story interesting if it hadn't happened to them? If the answer to that question is no, then writing it may be a worthy exercise for yourself but the likelihood of finding a larger audience is not great. That tends to be the biggest problem with the young writers.

DS: Just like young novelists or filmmakers. When you haven't had a great deal of experience, you draw on any intense experience you have had.

Study the Sensibility of the Producing Entity

DS: Now to change the subject. This is a specialized conduit, not the same as episodic network TV or feature movies. The quality of the language on "American Playhouse" is on a higher level. How does that work? Agents know this. Writers must know it. What would you recommend to a writer dealing with an organization like yours? What should they focus on?

LD: Well, I don't know if there is any formula. If you watch "American Playhouse" over a period of time, you'll start to see a certain sensibility emerge. We cover a pretty broad spectrum, from overtly political work to work that may raise political or social questions to the lighter comedies that may not be serious in tone. We are attracted to comedies that have something to say about the world or some insight to offer about human existence, even if they're doing that in a lighthearted way. That's what all good comedies do.

But I think the best thing to do with any organization that you're hoping to submit work to is to be as familiar with that organization as you can and to get as much information as you can. You can call here before submitting a script, either to me or to our assistant to the story department. We're more than happy to answer questions, listen to a quick pitch or say whether or not that sounds like something we'd be interested in. We have submission guidelines, viewer guides from the last few seasons.

DS: What are these submission guidelines?

LD: Well, ours are quite general because we do a broad range of work. The one essential ingredient for us is the American subject matter. We don't really state any philosophy in the guidelines. Our whole reason for being is to offer an alternative to what's being presented on network television, in commercial feature films and even on the commercial stage. We work with a lot of playwrights, usually those you see Off or Off-off Broadway.

DS: Do you think you are far more liberal in your attitude toward incoming work than, say, the networks?

LD: I think so. I think this literary department is even more open than a lot of theaters. Everything that is sent to us is given careful consideration. I read every page of everything that's sent to me. Everything is read in total by one of our reading staff.

DS: Let's talk about that for a minute. From the point of view of the writer, it's really gratifying to think that when you do send something, it actually gets consideration, because the general feeling is that this is a jaded industry. There's no question about that, based on my conversations with people from the "other coast," in many cases, to push a thing through you need not only high quality work but contacts and something monumental that makes you stand above the crowd. I imagine that's why you're doing this rather than working for the others.

How *does* a writer get through? Not just with a script—do they call, do they write to an agent? You have a dream you sculpt into a drama, a 120-page script, and it's quality, but you don't have an agent. What would you do?

Laying the Groundwork

LD: The first thing is to determine realistically which market is appropriate. I would say as a rule of thumb—there may be a rare exception—for a script that someone is sending to both "American Playhouse" and to a movie-of-the-week company— if it's right for one of us, it's going to be quite wrong for the other. And there's nothing more irritating for a development person than to get something that's completely inappropriate. I don't mind getting scripts that prove not to be right for us. We even get proposals for comedy series, a network comedy series, and those are the ones that you don't want to spend a lot of time on, because you know this person didn't even do the most basic research.

So the first thing is to realistically assess your market. The other is to get as many second opinions as you can. Playwrights do this all the time. I encourage writers to get people to read their scripts aloud for them — before they're submitted. It doesn't happen enough with television writers. If you're sending a finished script, then even if that script ultimately doesn't get produced, that's what is going to fix you in people's minds — that you're a writer to watch or not to watch so carefully. And I think all that groundwork should be laid before you expose yourself to the powers that be.

DS: Let's talk agents. How would you recommend getting an agent?

LD: Most agents, even at the major agencies, are more than willing to read the work of new writers, because it goes both ways — writers need agents, but agents need clients. Don't send a script cold to an agent. The best thing to do is send a letter and a synopsis of your script. And those count for a lot. We joke around here that you may not be able to judge a book by its cover, but you can often judge a script by its cover letter. People don't always pay as much attention to that as they should if they want to represent themselves intelligently, confidently, but not vainly and to show whatever knowledge they have of the organization. In any case, I think a good cover letter with an intriguing sounding synopsis of your script in most cases will get you an invitation from the agent to submit your script.

A Writing Sample

DS: Would you suggest, at least with beginning writers, that no matter whether they're dealing with a producer, an agent, or yourself, they finish a script rather than send a treatment?

LD: In most cases, yes. It's very hard for any organization — and I think we're more open to young writers than most commercial companies — to place its money and other investments behind the work of a person when you have nothing to go on. It is going to be very hard for me to get behind a treatment from someone who can't offer me a writing sample.

DS: But the writing sample could be something that had not been produced? No one can deny that you can't agree to give money to an unknown quantity, to actually spend a lot more money on production, unless you can see that they can write.

LD: One of my favorite scripts in development is actually a period piece — it's going to be more expensive than we are able to produce on our own. We'll have to raise money elsewhere. It'll be the first produced screenplay for this writer. But she had written several screenplays on spec. A wonderful writer, not writing in the commercial mode at all, so she had had some trouble finding productions for her work.

DS: How does a person like that survive?

LD: They teach!

Fees and Financing

DS: If a writer actually gets something through, how does she know what to ask for in terms of financing?

LD: It's quite simple with us. It's probably more complicated with commercial companies. We follow WGA [Writer's Guild of America]/PBS minimums, all across the board. If it's your first screenplay, we pay the minimum. If you're David Mamet, you're paid the WGA/PBS minimum. Keeps things very simple.

DS: Obviously, people don't do this to make a fortune.

LD: The figures we have to pay are small compared with what twenty-five-year-old graduates can earn writing sequels for the movies. People do come to us who have had commercial success. They come to us with projects dear to their heart in some way, and they know no one is going to pay them to write.

DS: If they don't come to you, where can someone go with your basic kind of project?

LD: Well, there are certainly independent producers, many of whom we work with. Often these producers will bring us difficult scripts that they really feel aren't going to get by elsewhere or that without our commitment they won't be able to find the rest of the financing. In many cases this is an accurate assessment, and with great regret we sometimes have to turn these projects down because they don't fit into any of our upcoming seasons, because we might have something too similar to it in development, or because we don't respond to it as passionately as the independent company does. We feel bad, and they're devastated because without us they can't get their film made. And then they go out and get it made anyway. I think as a writer it's more difficult. If you're going to write scripts that are more difficult, more specialized, perhaps even obscure, you may not find a large commercial audience. To find a director or producer who feels as passionately as you do about your work is absolutely essential. Those people will see it through, either by getting financing from overseas or by swinging home video presales, which is more difficult than it was three years ago but still an option.

Are Co-writers a Good Idea?

DS: Say you have a great concept and you're not yet a great writer—is there any point in attaching yourself to another writer, maybe an experienced one?

LD: I don't know that I would recommend that. It's different with commercial films that are more product oriented. We're very writer based. There have been occasions when people have co-written scripts, but it's not because one writer is weaker than the other. Right now, we have an American writer and a Soviet writer co-writing a script that deals with Americans in the Soviet Union, so there was a logic to that, and it's not that one writer is making up for the other's weaknesses. Each can bring something to the project. I would say that if you have reservations about your own writing and feel you need to work on your craft, the thing to do is to keep writing.

DS: Sometimes people can come up with great concepts but are not great writers.

LD: We are writer based to the point that if a script isn't going the way we want . . . When we put something into development it's because we expect to produce it down the line. We're not like studios that will put things into development and then let them sit on a shelf for five or ten years and maybe never get produced. We can't afford to do that; we just don't have the finances. But there are scripts that just don't turn out the way we wanted them to. Either it turns out that the writer's vision of the project isn't what ours was or it just proves to be more difficult. In those cases a commercial company, if they are still wedded to the idea of the project, will be likely to just fire the writer and get another one. We tend not to do that. In the overwhelming majority of cases, we would give the project back to the writer and let him do with it whatever he can.

DS: Basically, if someone does penetrate "American Playhouse," they can be fairly sure it's going to be produced?

LD: I would say that 85 percent of what we develop gets produced.

DS: Many Hollywood writers make a lot of money developing scripts that never get produced. Do you think that's better, because at least the writer is financially secure, or is it worse?

LD: I can think of nothing worse than writing and writing and never seeing the results of it.

DS: Let's get back to statistics. You're reading fifteen to twenty scripts a week. So all of you might be looking at fifty scripts a week. That's an enormous amount of material for one organization. Out of your fifteen, are there more good scripts currently? Has the writing gotten more sophisticated?

Technical Sophistication

LD: I think it's more technically sophisticated because there have been a lot more manuals published on screenwriting. People at least know screenplay form, which actually is quite important. The least you can do is deliver something that reads the way it's supposed to read. There seems to be more being written in general. When I started here three years ago, twenty scripts a week was a pretty average total submission to the organization. Thirty is now average and forty or forty-five is not extraordinary. Unfortunately, the fact that there are more being written doesn't mean that they're better. There are just more people writing.

DS: There are more people going to film schools than before. So, anyway, you have all these scripts—forty a week coming in from all over America — not just the two coasts?

LD: No. The heaviest concentration of them is from New York and Los Angeles, but we get them from everywhere.

Don'ts

DS: Okay, about 10 percent filter through, you said. What would you say would be the way *not* to break in; what is offensive? What would you advise writers to steer clear of?

LD: Don't send blatantly inappropriate stuff to us — you know, "slasher" scripts. Occasionally we get one and it just kind of shocks you. The next thing: There's a fine line between following through with a phone call or a letter to inquire about where your script is in the reading process and becoming somewhat of a pest.

When I get a script, I immediately send out a letter saying we've got it, are planning to read it, please be aware that the evaluation process takes eight to ten weeks, which is a pretty accurate assessment. And that's my way to avoid getting fifty calls a week saying, "Did my script get there?" Occasionally something really urgent will come up. Someone will say that they just got an offer on it, and "I wanted to know what you think." If it's a legitimate thing, I don't mind that at all. But sometimes after four weeks I get a call and I have to tell them, I'm sorry, I haven't gotten to it yet — and I get another call the next week. By the time week six rolls around, which is usually the time I'm getting to the script in my files, if I've already had three or four calls from that person wanting to know why I haven't read it yet — it's awful to say, but we're all human — you approach that script with fewer good graces than you might. Always respect the work loads of the people you're submitting to. It's completely natural and understandable for the writer; you've spent a year of your life on this thing, you've shown it to all your friends, it's the third draft, and you think it's the most important screenplay in the world — and you should feel that way. But you also have to understand our perspective: We have forty of those in the office; our resources are limited — we can't respond to everything quickly and not always in as much detail as we would like. I try not to send form letters, but there are times when I have to, just in order to get through the scripts that have accumulated in my office. That not only becomes the most expedient but the politest way of dealing with them, because it means that at least each writer will receive a response, whereas for a personal response, they may have to wait another month or two. Writers should understand that: When you get a form letter, it's not meant as a personal affront.

DS: Any more "don'ts"?

LD: This sounds incredibly mundane, but be sure to send readable scripts, scripts that won't fall apart, and make sure your address is on the script. These are little tiny things, but they're easy to attend to and make a good impression.

DS: So the concept of the wildly eccentric artistic genius doing anything he or she wants doesn't hold water in this environment?

LD: That's right. And it doesn't take much to attend to these basic details.

DS: Yes, if they can't do that minimum, it might be rather difficult to work with them.

LD: Also, don't send six scripts at one time. You start to think of them as a group and you keep putting it off. And I tell agents this too—some agents will send you eight different writing samples from eight of their clients—it's too much, and they're all being presented as if they carried equal weight. I think when agents do that it's a real disservice to their clients. Any one of those eight would be fine with me. When writers send their own work, they should choose the one or two scripts at most that they really think are appropriate for us and are the best examples of their work. If you send six, it's as if you were saying, "Oh, any of these will do." Again, it shows you haven't really done enough research to know which of the six is most likely to have real potential for us.

Best and Worse Case Scenarios

DS: Let's talk about an example of script that you remember that was unsolicited or didn't come through the normal channels or infrastructure.

LD: There are certain channels that everything goes through here regardless. One way of answering your question is to give the best and worst case scenarios. The worst is that it comes in, I send it out to a reader, a smart person who we trust. The reader sends it back—it has a very bad cover letter. I read ten pages or so, see that the reader is right and it goes no further.

DS: But you actually double-check it?

LD: In more cases than not. Again, if I look at what the cover letter says and it's clearly way off the mark for us and the reader hated it, I'm still compulsive enough to likely read a page or two of it. So that's the worst case scenario. The next step would be the reader recommends it, I read it, I don't like it. It goes no further. Next, I read it, I like it, but for one reason or another I know that it's something that isn't going to be right for us, in which case I would send the writer an encouraging note, thank him or her and encourage him or her to send other work. The next case would be a script that I like that I think could fit into our programming somewhere, which I would pass on to our executive producer or to the Director of Program Development for a second opinion, and if they like it and feel that it fits into the upcoming season, that it's something that we can produce for a reasonable budget, that it doesn't parallel something too closely we already have in development, then we would set about exploring how to go about producing it. If there is a director or a producer attached that's easier, because there's one other engine behind the project besides ourselves.

Truthfully, the number of projects we can commit to and have only a writer attached is somewhat limited. There are scripts that we'll feel passionately enough about that we will agree with the writer to find a way to produce their script. Then we'll go about with them finding the right director or producer to see it through production. But we can't do that with all eighteen programs each year, so in many cases it is to the script's advantage if there's some other engine behind it.

There was a script by a known writer who had not written for television before, but who had had a lot of stage work produced. We got the script from his agent. It was going to be produced that winter at a regional theater but hadn't yet been; he was a writer that we all knew. The agent just wanted us to see his latest work. We all liked it and decided we would find a way to bring it to film. So in that case we optioned the script.

DS: In that specific case, how long did it take from the time everyone read it and liked it to when it was on the air?

LD: It took a little while. Probably a little less than two years. And that was a case where we all felt strongly about the script, we could see a place where we could fit it in the following season, and we were willing to get behind it and do the legwork to find the right director, producer and studio.

DS: In the case of an unknown writer—they have an agent to negotiate the contract, they need that. Is there anything else a writer should do?

LD: Register it. I think also, just in terms of the larger picture, it's very important to be connected to the film and television community in some way.

DS: How do you do that?

LD: In New York, there's an organization called the Independent Feature Project, which is there basically to support beginning writers and to provide them with networks of people. I think the thing that makes screenwriting different from writing a novel is that it's by definition interactive and collaborative. You can sit and write a novel on your own and have that process work for you. I don't think it's true with drama. Whatever ways you can find to connect yourself to the larger community the better. Now New York or Los Angeles and other major cities all have [film] commissions, especially now that a lot of film production is taking place outside Los Angeles and New York—a lot in the South—so if you live in a state that seems to be off the track as far as commercial production goes, there's more than likely a film commission in the state that could furnish you with a list of upcoming productions. You could even get on-set experience, understand the process of shooting a screenplay, while also meeting other people in your field.

DS: Would you recommend that writers get their foot in the door by, say, trying it out as a secretary within the industry? I've always been skeptical about this, frankly. Or should writers just write and write?

LD: Many aspiring writers will work as production assistants as a way not only of supporting themselves but of keeping in touch with the world in which they want to work. The danger is that either you stay a PA and that may not lead to anything or you start moving up the production ladder and that becomes so absorbing that your other interests get put to the side. But that's an option. You can find other ways of supporting yourself that aren't related to the film world—which, in fact, can be much saner.

One of the dangers of film is it's so all-consuming. You're surrounded by other people who are thinking about the same things that you are all day, and you lose touch with what most of the world thinks about and worries about and feels in the course of their lives. I think it's very important to find some way of being in touch with other writers and working professionals so that people supply you with encouragement and support feedback. People can provide an example for you of how it's done and who can open those doors for you when you're ready to have them open. I really don't think you can sit at home, write, send your scripts off to people, get them back, write another script, and send it off to people again. I don't think it's a career that you can do through the mail. I think you have to be face to face with other people.

DS: People who will teach you something and help you get through. It's such a competitive world, this one. What would you recommend to avoid falling for myths? Keep turning up at a place?

Real Ideas, Real Passion

LD: I think it all has to start with the work. People ask, "What kind of scripts are you looking for?" What they mean is, "What should I write in order to get you to produce my script?" It has to start with the idea. Unless you have something you feel passionately about, you shouldn't be writing. You can knock on as many doors as you want to or work your way up, but if you finally get someone to listen to your ideas and you don't have the ideas, then you are wasting your time. This probably sounds soppy, but I do think you have to have that passion, an idea you feel an urgency about getting across, and a determination that film or television is the way you want to get it across. I think that is key, actually — I don't think it's a career you can go into half-heartedly. I think there are some jobs that you can take or leave. I don't think writing is one of those jobs. If you can think of three other ways that you can be just as happy supporting yourself, you should go do that because it's going to be a lot easier.

DS: Should a writer be thinking dispassionately about budget?

LD: With us it's a consideration. Most of what we produce falls between $500,000 and $1.5 to $2 million.

DS: Close to a movie-of-the-week.

LD: That's our high end. Most of our feature films fall between $1 and $1.5 million. Our TV projects are between $500,000 and $1 million.

Stand and Deliver

DS: Let's talk about your film *Stand and Deliver*. Was that written for you?

LD: Yes. This is a wonderful case scenario. Ramone Menendez and Tom Muska were two fairly young film school graduates. They had come across this article in the *Los Angeles Times* about Hymie Escalante, this totally inspiring Bolivian immigrant teacher who had managed to get a class full of barrio high school students to pass their math exam. And they thought this would make a great movie. They wanted to co-write it; Ramone would direct it and Tom would produce it. They had contacted Hymie Escalante, who sold them his life story for one dollar, and had done the groundwork, but they didn't want to write a script until they had a deal. Now they could have gone about it another way, but they chose not to. They shopped it around to all the studios. No success. They went to the networks, who had pretty much the same response. Who is going to watch a movie about a bunch of Spanish kids taking a math test?

Fortunately, they found their way to "American Playhouse" and Lindsey Law, who really deserves the credit. He said, "Great! Let's try it." They were very smart and promising but not greatly experienced. So they wrote it for us, and we paid them our standard fees. They did a first draft and a final draft with a set of notes in between, and then they really wanted to do it as a feature film, so they set about a way to do that. Even with a very fine finished script they met little response. We could only put in $500,000, and it cost a little over twice that. They got all their money from nonprofit sources: from us, from the Corporation for Public Broadcasting, from the Ford Foundation, the National Science Fund (it was about math), and they got money in the end from Pepsi, I believe. They pieced together their budget and shot the film. It was only after that the studios got interested. By this time they had Eddie Olmos, who had committed to the project quite early on, actually, and he deserves a lot of credit. Lou Diamond Phillips was cast before *La Bamba* was released, but by the time the film was completed he had become a young star. Suddenly the studios were very interested. By its first showing, the offers suddenly started rolling in.

DS: What are those two writers doing now?

LD: They spent a good year touring around gathering acclaim. They moved on.

DS: Was their writing based on their experience as well as the article?

LD: They're both Hispanic, and they were very tied to that experience and wanted to expose it. Warner Brothers released it theatrically first. Then we had the first TV airing with two versions, English and Spanish.

DS: A supremely good example of writers' intelligence. They saw something in the paper that was compelling and attractive.

LD: We paid them to develop it. They had a great idea and a

strong personal interest in it and a very clear conception of how they wanted to tell that story. Then they had the determination to go out and find a way to make it happen. They wouldn't give up. When they were fundraising, they sent out two hundred letters to foundations.

DS: Key stuff. A very severe persistence.

LD: Especially in independent film and public television. A lot of public television is where people pay out of their own pocket—a long, gruelling process. You've got to feel strongly. Persistence and passion and talent are the real keys.

One Executive's Sincerity

I think it is truly encouraging to see how dedicated and sincere Lynne is about her job and how much she cares. She reads everything she can and gives everyone, known or unknown, a fair shake. This reveals a lot of heart in a business that is not generally known for that quality. The dog-eat-dog image of big league showbiz is somewhat deserved, but there are still organizations like "American Playhouse" where quality writing is appreciated.

Also, Lynne's pointers as to the do's and don'ts of submission are valuable. She makes a big point of stressing that the worst thing you can be in your interaction with a group like hers is a pest. Her detailed exposition of her work load and how she handles it gives us a way of empathizing with the bureaucracy or a change. Sheer volume of submissions makes it almost impossible to respond immediately to anything. This helps us avoid a sense of personal affrontery when things don't go as quickly as we would like. It's worth knowing these things. It helps put the business into a more realistic perspective and takes the sting out of rejection.

Lynne also reconfirms that the main selling point will always be conviction and passion about your project. All the manipulation and cunning in the world does not add up to anything when it comes down to it: You have to love your piece, you have to be totally behind what you wrote and believe in its uniqueness and basic power, whether it be comedy or serious drama.

The overall impression I got from talking with Lynne was that

"American Playhouse" employees work very hard to find the best scripts out there. If you have something that fits their bill and you think it has the kind of high quality writing they are known for, send it to them. The worst that can happen is that you will get some very useful feedback.

Chapter Thirteen:

SUBMITTING WRITING TO CORPORATE AMERICA

WHEN NETWORK TV WAS IN ITS INFANCY, CORPORATIONS were the staple sponsors of television drama — Kraft, Chrysler and so on. In the late 1980s, this form of sponsorship returned in a big way. It seems that corporations now feel that, to keep the general public aware of their products, it makes a great deal of sense to sponsor high-budget television drama. Advertising agencies are the conduit for this corporate interest. They are responsible for the productions and work in league with established production companies or studios.

I thought that it would be interesting to discover the philosophy at work at these agencies vis à vis teleplay writers, and so I talked to Laura A. Mirsky, Program Development Supervisor at BBDO (Batton, Barton, Durstine & Osborne). Laura is the decision maker who presents scripts to her corporate clients for their backing and sponsorship for network distribution.

History of Corporate Sponsorship

DAVID SILVER: Tell me about the history of television dramatic production via the advertising agency, not necessarily just this one.

LAURA MIRSKY: Well, actually, it's sort of interesting because it gets to the heart of why I am where I am today, why we have a department here. As you may or may not know, in the early days of television, quite a lot of television production came out of advertising agencies. In fact, BBDO had television studios on the premises. We were a major supplier of programming to the networks—anything from "Armstrong Theater," "Texaco Theater" and "Kraft Showcase." Back in the early days, advertisers produced television specifically targeted at their buyers. Now that the networks are not as powerful as they were even ten years ago, now that viewers have all the other choices—cable, VCR home video—advertisers are getting back into the production business again.

DS: We're talking about the fifties originally for this?

LM: Yes, and it kind of stopped in the sixties.

DS: Why does the expansion of television outlets cause this to happen again?

LM: Money is more important again, frankly. If the Chrysler Corporation, which foots the bill for the "Chrysler Showcase," comes to the network with a $3.5 million budget, it's more important to them than it was ten years ago.

Clients' Images and Quality

DS: Give me a short list of your current clients.

LM: My three major charges are Campbell's Soup, Pepsi and Chrysler. Those are the three clients that I'm focused on now. Their programming needs are different and the way they work is quite different from each other. Chrysler and Campbell's Soup are both interested in the development of television movies. Pepsi is more oriented toward musical, rock and roll specials—youth-oriented stuff.

DS: So just in the same way that they entrust to an advertising agency the content and style of their commercials, is it right to say that they entrust the content and direction of their dramas to you?

LM: Well, yes. With Chrysler, the programming they're looking for is somewhat male-skewed, although not entirely, and I would say they're looking for things that are exemplary, uplifting—"event" television. Material that is going to attract major stars, male but not macho stuff—they don't want to do *The Dirty Dozen* —something that people are going to have a positive association with—for Chrysler automobiles. And as I said, since they're footing the bill, the projects Chrysler's going to do will have a bigger budget than most television movies, so we can afford to attract major stars.

For instance, one project we have in development at ABC right now has to do with preserving endangered wildlife in Africa. I think it would have been rather difficult to get that on the air, or to get it into development without Chrysler being behind it. James Garner is attached in one of the roles. I know that Turner Entertainment, for instance, is also developing a movie about a similar issue. I think Turner would be the more likely vehicle for this, if Chrysler weren't involved. So it's interesting. Although, yes, the product we're working on for the most part is commercial—it's not art house stuff—I think we're in a position to get quality programming on the air because we're not only interested in the bottom line; we're also interested in the clients' image. Naturally they're not going to want to get involved in anything that's bad for their image.

DS: So, in fact, rather ironically, a major corporation is more likely to put forward a quality program than, say, a production company.

LM: I wouldn't say it's more likely that they would put it forward, I'd say they'd be more likely to be able to do it, to get it done. And we don't work in a vacuum—we work with production companies.

DS: Okay, let's talk about that process in terms of how a writer would input into it. How does a writer enter this specific world?

A Tale of Two Scripts

LM: Well, there are all kinds of ways. I've got two movies now that we're developing from a script, which is unusual for TV as you know. Often things come from a book, a magazine article, a news story, from simply a concept. But we did get two fictional scripts from writers, one of whom has been writing for a long,

long time, has written several novels, and has just turned in a fabulous thriller script that's in development at NBC. Another script we've had in in-house development for a while is not set up in a network yet; that also came out of the brains of two writers, writing together, who hadn't done a movie-of-the-week before—it's a wonderful idea, and it can happen.

DS: That writer somehow knew about you and your infrastructure here and just got it right to you?

LM: One of them came from an agent and the other came through a producer who brought the script to us. It happens every way, it really does.

DS: What volume of incoming ideas do you have to deal with? I should preface this by saying that I can see about fifteen books, a lot of videotapes, papers, and piles of scripts piled on the desk here.

LM: I don't know. They come in every form and I'm always looking.

Seller's Market

DS: The prevailing mentality about all this is that people are just terribly hard to get to, that certain cliques exist, and that if you don't know the right agents and producers you'll never get through. This doesn't seem to be true. It's important for me to get this across—to communicate that there is receptivity. I'd like you to speak about that.

LM: Definitely. For good, appropriate material it's a seller's market, and people are scrambling all over each other to find it, to find the great stuff. It's tough to find great television, it's really tough, because what they're looking for is extremely prescribed, especially for network TV. It is beginning to open up quite a bit with all the cable networks. They're all doing deliberate counterprogramming to the networks, so that's making it interesting. We're trying to figure out a way we can do that for our clients, a way we can become involved in cable.

DS: So, in fact, you are not tied to the networks?

LM: No, we are trying to work with some of the cable networks, because I think they're doing very interesting things. If we can figure out a way, it'll make sense for our clients.

DS: But with not much direct advertising on the cable networks . . .

LM: But it doesn't mean that the clients can't have a part of the back end, for instance; that's already happening, even on the nonadvertising cable networks. I know for a fact that there's a movie on HBO that Bristol-Myers coproduced.

Don'ts

DS: Back to the writer. Let's talk about some do's and don'ts from your perspective — high-budget TV movies. What are some of the things that immediately turn you off?

LM: For my clients, I can't have anything terribly controversial, you know; I'm not going to get my clients involved in a lawsuit. It seems obvious, but it might not necessarily be. They are not going to get involved in anything sleazy. They're not going to do the Chippendale murders.

DS: They wouldn't do, say, a Roxanne Pulitzer biopic?

LM: There's no way.

DS: Okay, so that's in terms of taste. Let's talk more about quality and format. We're assuming that these major corporations do not want to be associated with bad quality or sleazy or litigious stuff. Let's talk about the writing quality. What are the things, as soon as you pick up the script, that you know are negative?

LM: Well, a personal thing that really turns me off is misspelled words. That sounds pretty silly, but it's an indication to me that someone is not paying attention. Now, things come in all different formats; if there's a germ of a great idea, it can be one sentence. But generally, things have to be fairly well fleshed out in order for me to present it to a client, for instance. Sometimes I'll do the fleshing out myself.

DS: That's interesting in itself. In other words, if a writer said, "Ms. Mirsky," if they're that polite, "I have this thing and it's about water pollution in the Midwest and there's a family involved," and they brought you that, just that, would you have some sense of what client to go to immediately with something like that?

LM: Sure, sure, absolutely. For instance, I'm working with a couple of writers right now who brought me a one-line idea, and I said, This is very cute. Two women—one had produced one thing for television and had never written; the other is a bestselling author who had never written for television. They did one treatment and I had problems with it. We had a meeting where I made suggestions, they did another treatment, I made more suggestions. I see things that are missing in it that they don't necessarily see. There was a very good germ of an idea there; I'm working with them on it to get it into shape, so I can present it.

DS: So by the time it gets presented, it stands a good chance?

LM: Yes. I think it stands a much better chance than when it was first presented. It wouldn't have flown. It had too many problems. That sort of thing happens all the time.

DS: Brian Siberell at HBO told me a similar thing. At the studios, however, they seem less open.

LM: Well, when I say, "It's a good idea but . . . ," it means that I don't like it. I probably shouldn't say that because it'll get me in trouble, but usually you're looking for a way to get out of it gracefully. I mean, you're not going to say, "I don't like this idea. Go away." You know what I mean?

DS: I do. But as a point of interest, shouldn't you tell someone honestly when they just don't have it?

LM: I'm usually not saying to a writer, "Don't write"—it doesn't usually come to that. It's more like, "This isn't for me." In the case I was talking about before, I thought the idea had commercial potential. Usually when I pass on an idea, it's not so much that it needs this or that. It's just that I don't see the commercial potential in it.

DS: If someone is as receptive as you, does it make sense for a writer to come in with a fairly skeletal idea? In other words, if you come in with the whole thing and someone doesn't like it, that's fairly intractable. If you come in with just an idea and say, "I want to do this film," then you have a lot of leeway.

LM: You need more than that. That's not quite enough. It depends on the kind of idea it is. If it's something that can really

be summed up in one line and make you go "Oh!" with one
line, then that's enough.

DS: Enough for what? Tell me about what happens after that.
One high-concept line and then?

LM: That's significant for television. It's much easier to sell that
to the network, that one line, and this is a cliché but it really
makes sense: Imagine the one line describing it in *TV Guide*.
It's really true.

DS: So a writer in the nineties and beyond has got to be something of a press agent too. How much so? Some people are so
slick about it all.

LM: That's never really appreciated.

DS: So how much should someone know about what's going on
in the industry?

LM: Well, I think it's good to know all you can but not necessarily
to be terrified by it. You can know so much that you're afraid
to do anything. Everything has been done, etc., in one form or
another.

DS: But if you had a great story about unrequited love, not about
pollution, violence, drugs, abortion, but just about a man and
a woman . . . ?

LM: You're getting to an important point. Casting. That's 75 percent of what gets a movie made on television. And it's difficult
with each of the networks, how important that is and the way
they do it. High concept and high-concept casting for TV is
very important. It can make a movie.

DS: When someone comes to you with a script that is good,
should they suggest casting?

LM: No. They'll never get it done, number one. Number two, let
us do it, because if you tell us something that's wrong, it can
kill it. We have one script—that's one of the cases I was telling
you about that came to us as a script—where we've attached it
to a major TV star at this point, and it'll probably get made
because of that. This particular network likes to use major stars
on their own shows, so we'll probably get a development deal
because of that.

DS: Not a surprise really. This is the way the industry works. Let's talk a little more about the process.

LM: I present to the client, and to the network as well. I'm also looking for material all the time. The publishing world, catalogues, lists from them. I meet with literary agents, screenwriters' agents, writers.

DS: Do you have a big staff?

LM: There are three of us plus a secretary. I read a lot of scripts and books, though not often whole books. I don't have time.

DS: Who buys the rights? BBDO?

LM: Sometimes the client and/or the production company and the network gets involved too. All together, really. It happens all different kinds of ways.

DS: I would have thought that if most writers knew about this particular conduit they would be very charged by it. How many writers know that you would be an excellent way to get a really good piece developed?

LM: Not that many writers know, I would say. Not that many people know yet. We're trying to make ourselves known as much as possible.

DS: You don't want a huge surge of stuff coming in, so maybe this is a nice position to be in.

LM: We're not the only ones any more. There are a few departments that have been in place for a while, but there are several new ones. In fact, at Young and Rubican they have a new department with the former development executive from ABC heading it up.

Corporate Involvement and Social Issues

DS: So major clients are now beginning to see that this may be a better way of advertising their products?

LM: It's a way to stand out from the advertising clutter, which is a big problem now. And it's a way to very particularly control the environment for their ads.

DS: Is all the advertising on a show from the main sponsor?

LM: On "Chrysler Showcase" it is. They buy the entire two hours from the network.

DS: Very compact.

LM: Hallmark does it. AT&T does it. IBM, General Foods, Procter and Gamble are getting back into the act. Each one is targeted in a slightly different way, which is nice, because it doesn't mean that we're directly competing with each other . . . except occasionally.

DS: You mentioned that Campbell's Soup was somewhat interested in social issues. Like what?

LM: Well, for instance, we have a movie coming up on ABC in spring called *Unspeakable Acts*, and it's a true story about child molestation in a day care center. It was a landmark case because it was the first time that the testimony of the small children was admitted as evidence in court.

DS: To me that sounds like a courageous show.

LM: It's excellent. It's very, very strong stuff. Chrysler is interested in that as well. Their movie about endangered wildlife in Africa is a social issue—*Mara*. I'm working on a project with a producer now that we're about to pitch next week about a Long Island fisherman who became fed up with not being able to fish in the Long Island Sound any more. He sued the town of Norwalk, Connecticut, and had himself eventually appointed as watchdog of the Sound, became an ecological activist; a man with no education and not a political sort of person—just a fisherman. I'm working on that right now.

DS: These are potentially explosive things in that could inspire people to activism.

LM: That's what we're hoping. At least to make people aware that they can clean up their own environment.

DS: This is interesting, the idea that major corporations are usually characterized as having a certain image, yet here so far we've spoken about projects that are distinctly socially conscious. You said that you couldn't get into too much controversy, but it seems to me you are defining controversy far to the left of normal, which is good. And all of this is very interesting from the point of view of the writer, as many writers, one way or another, get involved in things that are controversial. Writing comes out of suffering, disorder.

LM: Entertainment has to do with that as well. It's the kind of thing that television deals with well. When I say "nothing terribly controversial," you probably are not going to see us taking on the United States government.

DS: Or something pornographic. But in terms of issues that affect people and could inspire people to action—child abuse, pollution—this is very encouraging for writers. Do you think TV is changing radically? Entertainment was absolutely not defined in these terms until fairly recently. Is it a trend or will it go away?

LM: Good question. I don't think that this is going to replace true entertainment. I think you've actually seen these issue-oriented things on television for a few years now. Agent Orange movies, the Love Canal. TV does it well. Roe versus Wade. Though I don't think we would have been able to produce that. It was tough to get advertising for that show, I heard, but they did get it.

DS: From the writer's point of view, it seems to me that we're no longer in an age when the serious writer either writes novels or feature movies if he's lucky and forgets about television.

LM: No, not at all.

DS: I'd like you to talk about that.

Cable Blows Everything Wide Open

LM: Particularly with some of the cable outlets, who are very, very actively looking for controversial things—at least that's what they say. TNT especially. They want the small, controversial projects that an actor or actress can fall in love with. Faye Dunaway optioned *Cold Sassy Tree*—she's coproducing it, fell in love with it, wanted to play the part. It's a small story, the kind of thing that's hard to get on television these days—it can't be described in one line—but TNT is looking for this stuff. They come out and say that it's more important for them to attract attention than it is to get ratings.

DS: That's something of a turnaround, isn't it? Though these outlets never had the traditional attitude toward ratings.

LM: Then there are other cable networks that have gone the other way [advertiser directed] like USA; they're more bottom line than the networks in some ways. They're pure entertainment. Especially with their made-for-TV movies.

DS: So, in effect, because of the widening of the distribution spectrum there is diversification. Or is it just more of the same?

LM: They are diversifying very quickly with the advent of all the cable networks. And even more so now there's a big demand for material. Everybody is doing their own original movies now: Lifetime, USA, Showtime, HBO, The Family Channel, TNT, TBS, Nick at Night, Bravo, The Nashville Network, Cinemax, The Movie Channel, Disney — those are all new outlets, and a lot of them are doing movies.

DS: So it's becoming more like Britain, like Granada Television. They decided recently that it was better to make their own movies. They know they can sell them globally plus it gives them tremendous control.

LM: They coproduce with American television also.

DS: TV films are potentially global now.

LM: Absolutely global. This is one of the ways TV producers make money — by selling international rights.

DS: How long have you been doing this work?

LM: Four years.

DS: In those four years, what are the most significant changes you've seen?

LM: Cable. The advent of cable and home video. But cable is just blowing everything wide open, in terms of the venue for original movies. I think it still may be somewhat in the future that you see advertisers getting involved in series television, but that's starting to happen too. It's obviously much more expensive.

DS: But that's something that you can envisage your clients wanting to do?

LM: Possibly, yes.

DS: So a Chrysler or a Campbell's Soup or a Pepsi might even be interested in thirteen or twenty-six shows.

LM: Could be. If not a network, then in syndication.

DS: Obviously all these people now know you. How easy is it to get a writer's idea through to a major corporation with billions of dollars?

LM: Depends on the idea.

DS: What about the Long Island fisherman/activist idea?

LM: We're writing! I hope one of the networks will accept it.

DS: What about something that got through in the last two years?

LM: From the germ of the idea, and has been on the air?

DS: Yes. Process that. Typical procedure.

The Jessica McClure Story

LM: Let's see. There's no such thing as typical. The Jessica Mc-Clure story that came right out of the news — you know, baby Jessica. All the networks wanted it.

DS: Who got the rights to it?

LM: Campbell's Soup. With a production company. There were several producers involved for various reasons, and we made sure that the family was very well compensated, respected, well taken care of and not exploited. I think they knew, because it was Campbell's Soup, they weren't going to be badly treated, and we had the producers just make sure that all happened.

Another example is a movie that was on the air in December, 1988 on CBS called *Quiet Victory* about a man named Charlie Wiedermeyer, who was a high school football coach and contracted Lou Gehrig's disease. Nobody thought he would live, but not only did he live, he was able to coach his team to the state championship. This was a good experience for Campbell's Soup and for the family. At first, that was a story that everyone was all over, and then the networks wanted it. It was in development at ABC and then went to CBS, who put it on the air eventually. Nobody thought it would do well. There's always this thing: nobody wants a "soft" story, supposedly. We heard that this one was too soft — that's what we were getting. And then it won the night.

Unpredictable Successes

DS: In effect, you know when *you* want to do something; they know when *they* want to do something, but no one knows how successful it's going to be.

LM: Absolutely. That's absolutely right. And that's what's great about this business. There's a lot of luck. You've got to go on your instincts. Some people want to be totally commercial, that's just the way they are. God bless them. But if you've got an idea that you really love and you're fired up about it, chances are it's going to light someone else's fire too. It has to really excite you. "Gotta write . . ." I really think you've got to stay with the idea.

DS: Laura, do you find that people who deal with you, knowing that you represent big business — although you yourself are very human and approachable — still are determined to do their idea, not caring whether Chrysler or Pepsi likes it (they'd prefer that, obviously)? Are writers still artists or are they more like technicians now?

LM: Technique is art in my opinion. In TV? Writers are still artists. They have to be. I think craft *is* art. I don't think that it's easy. It's very hard to write a movie that works in the seven-act structure. Try it. It's very hard!

A Slice of the Corporate Pie

If you are really serious about writing for television, then you have to examine all the possible doors of entry. Here we have the quintessential corporate situation where one would imagine the only job would be writing ingratiating advertising copy. It is fascinating to see that three major corporations have backed, through BBDO, worthwhile projects involving high-quality writing. I am not sure how receptive BBDO would be to completely new writers, but you can see from the interview that new writing "product" is always being sought by the powers that be. Laura Mirsky seems to be very open to reading anything and everything that comes her way in her quest for suitable material for her major clients. We also see that serious social issues are becoming one of the staples of feature movie television, even those sponsored by pillars of the capitalist establishment.

Another key lesson is that the writer has to be very clear as to who buys what. Just by studying Laura Mirsky's words, we can see that BBDO's clients want serious, somewhat unspectacular fare. Pollution and environmental conservation are crucial issues for the nineties, but they are not sensational, so writers wanting a slice of the corporate pie should definitely concentrate on this kind of subject matter. It may not be the way you want to go, but reading the interview will also let you know that the expansion of distribution outlets is a very real phenomenon and assures writers a broader market to investigate and use to their advantage.

Chapter Fourteen:
THE PAY
CABLE SCENE

THROUGHOUT THIS BOOK, WE HAVE HEARD REFERENCES TO THE broader market available to the new writer, making the nineties a much more fertile ground than earlier decades. The most important component of this expanded TV universe for the writer is unquestionably pay cable TV. After the first flush of success, where it was sufficient for the major pay cable networks just to show features six months after their theatrical releases, it became necessary to create original movies.

The New Cable Universe

By the late eighties, HBO had been in the business as a strong player for fifteen years. They led the way all down the line in the institution of good quality, feature-length movies made for television. Suddenly, fiction television writers had whole new sets of dramas to fantasize about as their stomping grounds. Every year there are many new places to attack as a goal for professional writing. It is still a major struggle to actually get something of yours developed and produced, but the odds are better now that if you have an outstanding idea and script you will be able to get it through the new bureaucracies who make the decisions.

Cable network executives are younger, hipper and more open to the writing of their contemporaries. Obviously, you still have to write terrific stuff and combine that with a strong, correct pitching approach.

I talked with Brian Siberell, who's director of HBO's " HBO Showcase," the most prestigious of the pay cable series single dramas. Brian used to be an agent, but at a fairly tender age moved on to become a decision maker at the most established of the pay cable networks. He is open, very bright and genuinely interested in pushing the quality of the medium further, to more exciting places. My conversation with him is multileveled; Brian not only explains Home Box Office's philosophy of submission, selection, development and production, but he also gives us useful insights into the state of pay-per-view cable, television in general and the immediate future potentials of the medium.

History of HBO

DAVID SILVER: Could you give me a tiny history of HBO and "Showcase"?

BRIAN SIBERELL: HBO celebrated its sixteenth anniversary, so we're into our seventeenth year right now. "HBO Showcase," which is this series of single dramas, has been in existence since 1986. The first one was called "Half a Lifetime." It was adapted from a Stephen Metcalfe play. We've done about nineteen or twenty single dramas. We knock off about six or seven a year.

DS: What is different about "Showcase"? Were there any original dramas on HBO before?

BS: There had been a few original dramas but they were sort of scattershot, and they weren't collected under one unifying umbrella. They had success with two separate dramas. One was "Mr. Halpern and Mr. Johnson," starring Laurence Olivier and Jackie Gleason and written by Lionel Goldstein. The second was a Robert Altman adaptation of Marsha Norman's "The Laundromat" with Carol Burnett. So these were self-contained single dramas rather like "Playhouse 90," "Studio One"—that sort of very, very intimate material, you know, actors doing what they do best on television. We were hoping to return to that sort of tradition.

DS: Lionel Goldstein must have been a mite pleased at the stars they got for his first TV drama!

BS: Yes, it was his first. You can imagine his astonishment to get Gleason and Olivier to be in his first production.

DS: How many "Showcase"'s have you been involved with?

BS: About sixteen of them.

The Search for New Writers

DS: How diverse has the search for writers been?

BS: We look for new writers about as much as anybody does in this country. My own background is a theatrical one. We really scour—we don't just rely on network approved writers' lists; in fact, we don't even have one. That's not the way we work. We do like to work with people who have written screenplays in the past or simply plays or television. We'll take talent where we find it, but we certainly cover the regional theaters, cover the New York theaters. I try to make it my business to look at everything that comes out as a feature release. We also cover the U.K. a good deal.

DS: So it's not just a question of stuff coming through agents?

BS: No. I also speak on panels like the one you and I met on at the New York Writers' Conference. I take a look at who's coming out of schools. I read all the press releases that come in. We try to keep up with all that's going on out there. In that regard, HBO's not a closed shop at all.

DS: That's obviously very good to hear, but let's get to a very fundamental question. What is the minimum you would look at before you could say, "We're interested"? Is it a concept, a treatment, a fully written script?

BS: I'm happy to read a treatment. The difficulty is, if I read a treatment or even a two- or three-line concept that sounds quite interesting to me, I'm then going to want to see a screenplay which gives me an indication that this writer has the chops, you know. Whether he or she has written for television in the past isn't so important as do I know they can do it. If we're going to be the first one to give them a shot, I need some examples of their work so I know they can do the job.

DS: But say, hypothetically, they have something—something else written. You would look at it?

BS: Absolutely.

DS: In point of fact, talking over the range of the twenty or so "Showcase"s HBO has produced, approximately how many of those came to you from someone who hadn't written lots of teleplays already, people very early on in their TV career?

BS: In fact, a great many of them were fairly early on in their career. Ten out of the twenty hadn't really had much experience in TV as such.

DS: So 50 percent were neophytes, at least in television?

BS: Yes. They had perhaps written for the theater before this but never for television.

DS: It seems to me that HBO is fairly open in this regard. Are you more open than the networks?

BS: I would like to think that we are. Networks and many large companies have approval lists because there's a certain pool of writers whom the networks like. We, because we're trying to do something different and distinguish ourselves from everything else that's out there, have to move a little quicker, taking perhaps a few more risks. We have to work with writers who are not really right for the networks, because the kinds of things *we're doing* are not really "right" for the networks. We try to be more clever. Consequently we don't rely on people who've done things before. Someone who's done three or four movies-of-the-week isn't necessarily the kind of writer we want to have anyway.

DS: So this is really an aesthetic and somewhat intellectual decision rather than a financial one, because the budgets are relatively similar.

BS: Our budgets are somewhat smaller, in fact. That in itself is an aesthetic decision.

Budget Awareness

DS: When a writer submits a piece to you, a fully written screenplay, how aware are the writers of the budget, as a rule?

BS: Some more than others, but I've never had a case where I've worked with a writer and I've said, "Listen, fella. You know, we can't have three laser swords here, and take out that car crash." I've never had anyone say, "I simply insist upon that." I've found all the writers we've worked with have been very easy in that respect. However it is true, David, that someone will send in a script after I've spoken to them and told them point blank the sort of things we're financially capable of, and then they'll send me a script with car crashes all over the place or cars going the wrong way down Sunset Boulevard or something. They're clearly not thinking.

Quality and Controversy

DS: I don't think anyone would disagree that HBO has fairly high standards in terms of scripts, like *Tailspin*. The scripts are more concerned with issues that are sort of controversial.

BS: You see, pay cable has the freedom to do that because we're not reliant upon advertisers to put our product together. A thing like *Tailspin*, for example, took a different tack than what NBC took on their show *Shootdown* [both films about the shooting down of the Korean passenger jet] — theirs was quite good, mind you, but we all read in the papers about the sort of compromises that were necessary to please NBC's parent company. If you look at HBO or other pay cable organizations that don't rely on advertisers, you're going to find a great deal more freedom. They love a little controversy. They don't run away from it; they welcome it.

DS: Nevertheless, HBO is a massive company by now and it's not as if a cavalier attitude is at all possible.

BS: Granted.

DS: Okay, if one is a writer and one has a piece that, let's say, is reality based, would the writer stand a better chance sending it to HBO than, say, Tri-Star or NBC?

BS: It's difficult to make a blanket generalization.

DS: Let's be specific. Remember NBC's *Wallenberg* with Richard Chamberlain? A great show — that would seem to be an HBO-type show now.

BS: Sure. HBO had something else in development, the Simon

Wiesenthal story, which we did make. They cut across one another. Those are examples of where television can do its most good.

DS: So you feel that a writer can think of your receptivity in terms of some form of idealism?

BS: Idealism tempered by reality.

DS: Sure, but not out-and-out crass "We don't care about idealism—just give us the heavy ratings"?

BS: Ratings are important, but not of paramount importance. Pay cable is trying to sell subscriptions, and to do that, it's not so much a question of how many people are watching tonight but more how many people read about it the next morning, plus the word of mouth on the show afterwards. Then people who don't have HBO feel that they should be subscribing, and they'll sign up. That's what it's really all about. Not how many eyeballs are watching the set.

DS: What would be your advice to writers submitting work to HBO and the like?

BS: People should be going through an agent. If they don't have an agent, they should certainly get a lawyer. We do have an agreement which we'll send out to unsolicited manuscripts— basically a waiver, which is standard in the industry. I think that here we're quite open like most of the big cable companies, because again, they have to offer something different from business as usual. The programmers are much more adventurous. They have to be.

What's Right for Network is Wrong for Cable

DS: What would be some of the "don'ts" about submission? What immediately says "red light," "I don't want to deal with this script"?

BS: I do want there to be a cognizance on the part of the writer as to what the budgetary limitations are. I want the writer to be aware of what pay cable can offer as against what the networks have to offer in terms of content and approach. Oftentimes we will get a script which is perfect for one of the networks to do. You know, it's a really great "artificial insemination" story, something like that. That's for them, and they should go to them with that. The word around here is if it's great for network television, then we don't want it and vice versa, generally. Obviously, I want something literate and well written. But the sort of things we produce tend to be edgy and contemporary, so if someone submits a story about unrequited love in the twelfth century, it's not going to be quite up our street. Someone can learn that quite easily by calling me up and asking me.

Many Avenues of Approach

DS: So you want contemporary stuff, but not milk and water. Let's talk more specifically. Choose one of the dramas on this roster of yours — the most recent, or one with a writer who isn't super well known. I'd like to know how it got to you, from the very start.

BS: Andy Wolk is a writer I had wanted to work with, and one day he told me about an experience he'd just come off as a juror in a murder case — a murder in a crack house. That got us talking about drugs and the criminal justice system — both urgent issues — and we said, "There's a great movie here." We commissioned a script and that turned into *Criminal Justice*, which Andy wrote and made his directorial debut with.

DS: You mentioned that HBO has done about twenty single dramas. How many of these twenty would you say came straight from the writer, then?

BS: Just a few.

DS: And they called you or your secretary on the phone and said, "I have something. Will you talk to me?"

BS: Yeah. Only one had a great track record already; the others were just breaking out.

DS: Had they fully written these scripts before they came to you?

BS: One of them, yes; the others, no.

DS: So that suggests to me a certain kind of flexibility. There aren't any ironclad rules.

BS: No, indeed. We're not looking for fully finished screenplays. It would be the greatest thing in the world, though, if I could find ten camera-ready scripts on my desk. But that's not the way you do it, you know—it's a long, difficult process.

DS: For a writer with that kind of entrée, which is not incredibly highfalutin—you know, you liked it and you connected—would you recommend a modus operandi of payment, remuneration for a writer? Do you suggest the writer work it out for him- or herself? What about lawyers, agents, normal procedure? What should the writer do to ensure a fair deal?

BS: Either/or, lawyer, agent. I would ask, Who speaks for this person? Generally it's to our mutual benefit that he or she has representation of some kind who already knows the ropes and is familiar with the rules.

DS: In terms of fees for the relatively new writer, is there a lot of latitude or is it pretty much scale?

BS: Perhaps it's quite different elsewhere, but here there's not so much money involved that there's a wild variance of fees.

DS: And prospective writers should talk to an agent who's dealt with you before?

BS: I needn't have dealt with the agent before, but it should be a franchised agent.

DS: Tell me more about approaches to you.

BS: A director, producer, even the writer comes to you with something of a track record. You prick up your ears. That's no mystery. That does not preclude us from looking at people who don't have much of a track record, but there's no doubt that if you're on the fence about something—you're somewhat titillated but not convinced—the presence of someone who actually has a real track record which you like and respect—that just may push it over.

DS: At HBO, how many people read the scripts?

BS: Besides myself, there are two other people here and we employ two readers, but they're not full time. We do a heckuva lot of reading ourselves.

DS: That's rather surprising, given the size of HBO.

Trends for the Nineties

DS: Taking a different tack for a minute. As an ex-agent, just looking at it as broadly as you can, for the last sixteen years since HBO's start, do you think writing has improved on the whole?

BS: Of course there are very good writers around. Whether the writing is up to the standard of thirty years ago, I'm unsure. There was a time when the real writers' tradition came out of theater — the Paddy Chayevskys, Rod Serlings, people like that. However, though I bring up Serling's or Chayevsky's name — they're totemic, aren't they? We remember because they *were* so good — the fact is that there were probably a lot of bad writers in those days too. We choose not to remember them. People deride and dismiss television all the time, but the fact is that there's a lot of good stuff going on. If you watch enough of it, you can see that. There's so much more stuff.

DS: On the whole, discounting people who are way off the mark, the stuff you receive — how good is it?

BS: There are a lot of tremendous writers. That's not at all to say that we don't need more.

DS: What is your feeling about the future? What are the trends that might be happening in the nineties?

BS: Well, society is changing radically. Life as we knew it is not going to be at all the same. I'm not sure that entertainment is reflecting that, and it's going to have to. Like it or not, it really is a new world. All sorts of new media are being created to reflect that world and I don't think we should be thinking backwards. I don't think we should be putting on the same traditional sitcoms and dramas which have worked in the past. There clearly have to be new forms. When you look at some of the television that's working now, it's getting more subversive; it's getting a little wicked. Those are the kinds of shows that will take us into the next few years. If indeed there are no new stories and if indeed everything's been said, then you have to say it in a new way. It's that simple.

DS: Are you feeling these currents now in terms of what is being submitted to you?

BS: Not enough yet. Hope springs eternal.

DS: You get a lot of scripts. What are people writing about now? What keeps coming up?

BS: Pretty much domestic dramas or crime thrillers. That reflects the success of some of the things in the marketplace already. People see a trend—*Fatal Attraction* does well, *Sea of Love* and *Black Rain* do well—more thrillers get written. If domestic drama does well, then there's a wave of those. Whether these are scripts that people have in their minds already or they were on the shelf just waiting to get on, I don't know.

DS: I see *The Big Easy* with Dennis Quaid was on network recently—a pretty raunchy film. It's been on HBO and has been rented heavily. Not as much differentiation between pay cable and network now. Is this happening?

BS: There have always been movies made in Hollywood which eventually end up on the network. The end view is not as crucial as what is being specifically made for the primary market. Is everybody making the same stuff? No, I have to disagree. It behooves programmers competing with thirty or so channels to do what no one else is doing. It seems smart for individual producers and programmers to come forth and say, "Hey, look at me! My stuff is different from the next guy's." This is starting to happen already. Disney, HBO, Turner.

An Agent's Functions

DS: How does that impact on the writer? Should a writer really be focusing: "This is HBO and this is what they want," "This is ABC; this is what they want"?

BS: I think that's what an agent is for. First of all, I do believe that people who write for television should watch some television. Not for bad habits, but rather to educate themselves as to what's going on. And quite often writers who want to work for television heap nothing but opprobrium and scorn on the medium, which is stupid. Just stupid. It's self-defeating. You have to dig TV, you have to want to improve it, you have to want to do better than the last guy. You have to have an affectionate respect for the medium.

I think it helps any artist to have some sort of understanding of the marketplace.

On the other hand, it can often be destructive to one's art to know too much. So whether one is going to be spending all one's time going to feature movies or watching Disney, watching Turner, Showtime, HBO, the three networks, Fox and trying to peg everything he or she wants to write upon that particular outlet—I'm not sure that's a good thing. It may have a corrupting effect.

But that's what managers and agents and lawyers are for. I mean, a good agent provides that kind of advice. A good agent knows what the market is looking for. And that's why agents are good, not simply because they can negotiate contracts, but rather because they act as counsels for the artists.

DS: What is the best way to find a good agent?

BS: I'm quite certain that the Writers' Guild already publishes a list of authorized agents. Okay, that's one step. Secondly, think about whether you know any writers represented by agents; do they recommend them? A third step is to take a look at some writers you admire, just for fun. Call the Writers' Guild and find out who represents them.

DS: None of that is confidential?

BS: No, no, no. And then start knocking on the doors, start calling. You obviously should have something to show these agents, and it should be something that's not only impressive artistically but it should be something they can sell as well. That's what the agents are doing in the business.

DS: Pressing an agent is like pressing an executive. Do you have any words of wisdom about that?

BS: Well, I'm a real sucker for a good cover letter. The writer's forte is the printed word, and most agents respect that. Otherwise, they shouldn't be in the business. A letter of introduction might begin, "Hi, I'm so and so," you know, "I'm not a complete novice, but I'm just not represented. Here's what I'm about, here's where I'm from, here's what I've written ... I would love very much if you could take a look at this, and perhaps I could come in and meet with you." If that's an impressive, well-written letter, believe me, it should work. If someone's paying attention, it'll absolutely work. And you would be surprised at the number of writers who don't quite seem capable of that, who underestimate the worth of a really good letter.

DS: Would you recommend a writer go through an agent rather than a production company; for instance, this company's done a certain number of TV films that I recognize as being somewhat similar to the one I've written?

BS: Well, the truth about the business is what William Goldman said: "Nobody knows anything." So for me to say that it's a better idea to go to a production company with an agent in tow, I dunno. There are no maps provided you; you have to try everything. And I'm very sensitive to the Catch-22 of [the situation]: an agent won't represent you unless you've done something, but you can't do anything unless you get an agent. But the fact is that the world is flooded with writers who are doing something, who do have agents, so, clearly, there's a way to get over. And you can't just be content to sit back and say, "Oh well, they made their connections at a party in Amagansett." That's not the way things are really done. The fact is it's just hard work.

DS: The people out there who have absolutely no access in any case to parties in Montauk or Bel Air, but live in Iowa or Oregon or somewhere . . . ?

BS: No, but they can get to the Iowa's Writer's Workshop for instance, or maybe they have to sleep on Aunt Bea's couch in Brooklyn Heights for three or four months and come to New York and kind of educate themselves as to what is going on. I'm certain there are great writers in Omaha. There are certain systems to come up through, whether they are university sponsored, whether they began publishing locally or what have you. I mean, you start small.

Respect for Writers

DS: Once you have gained some interest, what modifications should a writer expect, and not be surprised by, before any money is spent on production?

BS: Except for a very few writers, it's no secret that in America film is really regarded as a director's medium. In fact, this is true all over the world. While the writer is of great, great import, much of television is really a producer's medium: In a series, you have a lot of writers working on the same thing at the same time. There is respect but not reverence accorded the writer in the States. It's different in the U.K., where so many writers come from the theater. There's a reason for that. If you look back to the foundations of Hollywood, the fact is you'd have eight or ten really great writers all working on the same stuff—Ben Hecht rewriting Faulkner or something. So people do get rewritten in this business. Writers do feel yanked around all the time. And a lot of good ones too. They're asked to do things that they're not always that willing to do.

But that's not the way it has to be. I mean, depending on the executive, the studio and the network; most of them have great respect for the writer. It's also true that the writer is asked to be the most flexible of the collaborators. It's a collaborative medium anyway. You get the director, the producers in there, the actors, the executives, all of whom may have different notions of what the thing ought to be. The writer should remain open, but should stick to his guns when he or she thinks it's important to the integrity of the project. But it's not like writing for the theater, where a writer can maintain great authority.

New Boundaries in TV

DS: In terms of salability and aesthetics, what are the things you can tell a writer he or she can do in the early nineties that perhaps couldn't be done before?

BS: There's no question there's a great deal more freedom of content than ten or fifteen years ago. You look at some of the stuff on TV and scratch your head and say, "Holy cow! I can't believe they are doing this on television!" So the boundaries are always being pushed back. Look at the style of videos and how they've revolutionized the storytelling process on TV. "Miami Vice" came out of MTV-style innovations. So there are changes taking place.

DS: But, Brian, even though one thing might jump forward, most things seem to stay pretty much the same. Like "Hunter"-type episodics — primitive, conservative.

BS: But "Hunter" is not presented as an innovative pioneer . . .

"HBO Showcase" Examples

DS: Back to HBO. Choose a couple of your "Showcase"s that would indicate a way that a writer can operate now which is closer to his or her primary vision without being truncated.

BS: Well, *Tidy Endings* had originally been one act of a three-act play written by Harvey Fierstein, and that wasn't messed with at all in terms of content. I think that would be a very good example of a writer's vision that was realized, enhanced by the director but not distorted. *Fellow Traveller* was a screenplay about the McCarthy era blacklist written by a first-timer, Michael Eaton. He had hoped for a modest little taped studio drama. Next thing he knew, we had optioned his script, put a co-production deal together with the BBC and the BFI [British Film Institute], and brought on board director Philip Saville. We shot it on 35mm and it played in the U.K., where it became a hit. So forget talk about limiting a writer's vision — in most cases, we enhance it. With both of these shows, I would argue that the result was what the writer was trying to bring it to.

   Conspiracy: The Trial of the Chicago Eight was certainly rather risky in content and form.

DS: Was that based entirely on transcripts from the court?

BS: Yeah, but it was actually a very interesting blend of dramatic re-creations of the court transcripts, talking heads' reminiscences of the participants today, newsreel footage from the day, period music . . . it was all blended together in this wonderful tapestry that worked very, very well, I thought.

DS: So that was a true docu-drama? Was it commissioned?

BS: No, it was developed for one of the networks — I don't recall which one — and it couldn't get on. They fell out of love with it for whatever reason, but it was perfect for us.

DS: Was it as groundbreaking in terms of its interesting structure when it was originally developed for the network?

BS: Well, we realized it, but we didn't develop it. Jeremy Kagan brought it to us. It was a fully written script. Now there were some changes made, no question about that, but what we put up on screen was pretty much what had been on the page.

DS: So he had a late eighties Abbie Hoffman plus a fictionalized Abbie?

BS: Oh yes.

DS: Well, that kind of project acceptance is very encouraging. Final question. Bring us up to date with something you've just done, something from a new writer and the process it went through to get to you and so on.

BS: We've just produced a film called *One Man's War*. It had been in development for quite a long while, in fact. It's a true story of a torture and murder in Paraguay under the Stroessner regime, the story of a doctor who was a very vocal critic of the Stroessner regime. His son was tortured and murdered by security forces within that country. It's the family's fight to bring the killers to justice.

DS: Who wrote and directed that?

BS: Michael Carter, an English writer, and Sergio Toledo, a Brazilian director.

DS: How did he get his source material? Did he go to Paraguay?

BS: In fact, in the quest to bring the killers to justice, which eventually they did do, Amnesty International got involved, and this was pulled from their files. We thought it was very interesting, powerful stuff and lent itself very well to dramatization. The family was also very cooperative.

DS: Thanks for talking to me, Brian.

Footnotes

This interview is interesting because it displays two seemingly opposing aspects simultaneously. Brian is extremely pragmatic and hard-nosed about the rigors of getting a script developed or bought by HBO. At the same time he shows that this most important pay cable chain is genuinely looking for new material, material with bite and strong content to boot.

The burgeoning cable drama industry is a thoroughly good

thing for new writers. As Brian puts it, they are in the business of discovering new ways to grab an audience, of outwitting the networks. This entails being open to new work and innovative, fresh writing. The professional writers, approved by networks and prestigious supplier production companies, always have the potential to create hackneyed, cliché-soaked stuff that is not acceptable for the cable players. This is very encouraging indeed for the new writer. Yes, you still have to be able to deliver a story with a commercial dimension firmly in mind. HBO and Showtime cannot tolerate financial insecurity any more than can the networks. But the logic of their competitiveness with the networks necessitates a more liberal attitude toward new writing. If it is good and will bring more subscribers to the cable network, then it will be looked at very seriously. This means that the "closed shop" theory of TV writing has less validity — as long as the cable programmers and buyers want to keep a step ahead.

There are simply more places to go. Brian Siberell makes it quite clear that HBO is very open to new, significant work. The old rules are breaking down, and fairly quickly too. There will be many more original dramas from pay cable in the nineties as they see the cost-effectiveness of producing their own movies and owning them down the line, so that it works out much more beneficially financially to own rather than rent, as it were. The cable boys are beginning to see big bucks in original production, the many ancillary benefits, including home video sales. This all bodes well for determined TV writers.

Conclusion:
WRITE,
WATCH,
WRITE

To BECOME A GOOD WRITER OF ANY SORT YOU HAVE TO WRITE as much as you can to perfect your skill; watch the world and watch yourself to constantly mine new material, then write more based on your new observations and feelings.

To become a successful working television writer you have to write, watch and write, as I just said, plus you must also watch television and observe the industry. Other sorts of writers need not pay as much attention to the commercial marketplace. Novelists do not usually pay much attention to current trends in publishing; good playwrights write directly about what they feel and think about the universe and the human condition. But it is essential for TV writers to be very aware of the television industry.

TV Is Getting Better

In an article in the October 7, 1990, *New York Times* Arts and Leisure section entitled "Yesterday's Boob Tube Is Today's High Art," Randall Rothenberg makes a case for the elevation of prime time television fare into something approaching art, involving an auteur theory of creativity and execution. With tongue slightly in cheek, Rothenberg suggests that TV has more going for it artistically than most people would think.

Newer producer/writers like Steven Bochco, he feels, create

deeper and more relevant work than TV is known for, and this quality can even be traced back to shows like "Dragnet" from the fifties. He quotes David Marc, a visiting professor at the Annenberg School for Communication at the University of Southern California: "There are distinctive voices speaking on television, which gives the lie to the thought that it's a single, monotone, hegemonic voice." Creators like Stephen J. Cannell ("The A-Team," "The Rockford Files," "The Greatest American Hero"), the article implies, do more than mass produce pulp viewing. They also put part of themselves into the shows, just like a novelist or film director.

Even if Rothenberg's case is a little exaggerated, the truth is that TV is definitely getting better, and this means that the desire to become a professional TV writer does not automatically make you a hack. I want you to remember this as you embark upon TV writing as a profession. It will keep your aims high and will ultimately improve the overall quality of the medium. More important maybe, it suggests that you can prepare quality material and not necessarily be dismissed out of hand by the people who make the decisions in TV land.

Balancing Creativity and Pragmatism

Television writers, in order to get their visions on the air, must pay attention to what is actually on television. This applies more to fiction than nonfiction, though even in any realistic appraisal of getting documentaries made, there has to be some current knowledge of what is getting funded.

For either kind of writer, to be obsessed with what seem to be the current trends is dangerous and basically undesirable. I have met so many people in New York City and Los Angeles who know just everything there is to know about what's going on in TV. Yet this detailed knowledge does not give them what it takes to actually write television programs. So, while stressing the necessity to keep abreast, I would warn against too much brooding over what you can do to dovetail into the current video fads and fashions.

The decision makers I talked to stress that a combination of skills is essential: talent plus clear business sense. On top of this I maintain you must also strike a subtle balance between doing your own thing—writing what you want—and knowing what stands a decent chance of being bought. It is not the easiest and most pleasant state of mind to nurture; however, as in any other rewarding but hard task, those are the breaks.

If you just want to write TV movies and programs that you can only fantasize will get on the air, that's another matter. There is nothing wrong with that—one of these innovative, explosive pieces gets on the air every so often, and that is worth fighting for if that is your bent. But if you have read this book because you want to become part of the mainstream of TV creators—and I suspect that is what most of you do want—then you have to keep up this double whammy game of balancing on the one hand what people in industry will be able to "get," and maybe even develop and produce, and on the other, the products of your pure creative fire.

I am loathe to deter people from fighting to get their dreams on television. I have done it all my working life. Just remain realistic and cogent about what the real odds are against getting anything on television in a culture dominated by the dollar, fueled by sponsorship, and funded by corporations, foundations, networks and so on.

Confidence and Energy: Your Hidden Assets

One of the qualities I repeatedly emphasize is confidence. It might seem more appropriate to stress ways to persuade agents or producers, or tricky methods to ingratiate yourself with decision makers. But I genuinely feel that it is better to urge prospective artists-in-media to work on their confidence level and energy preservation. It is so easy to be beaten by the television game with its contorted paths to execution and fruition; to be oppressed by repeated rejections and paranoid feelings that all the work goes to others, people you rarely meet who in some intrinsic and mysterious way are not like you. This fear is actually the major obstacle to success.

Yes, it is hard. Yes, occasionally it is horribly annoying. Yes, I have to admit that every so often it is a thoroughly nauseating business. I am sure people in gems or in shipping or in garments or in stationery manufacture say exactly the same thing. Business is business. It does not have the same valence or charge as the art itself. Creating is a very private, beautiful thing, somehow inviolate, always rewarding in itself. The trade part of art, though, can frequently be downright depressing—people steal ideas, they put yours down and then use them somewhere; you experience all manner of craven activity in the back rooms of the television world, etc., etc. Despite all that, good work gets on television. It isn't all dreck, and the players are not all sharks.

So, keeping up the energy level of your participation while quietly, realistically preserving your confidence is an essential part of the discipline. I know from personal experience that when I allow my confidence to fade and even wither, there is little hope of actually getting my work on television. It is just too fierce a battle to allow for intense feelings of failure or lack of self-esteem as a writer. Somehow you have to keep on smiling through the dance of rejection, initiation, maintenance and possible success. In order to keep on making it happen and not buckling under the pressure of that, you have to involve yourself seriously in the self-discipline of creating work regularly, even when you are not selling your stuff. Keep at it—daily if possible—and see your work mature and improve. Then move even more deftly toward the agents, producers, story editors and foundation funding people, standing a better chance of success each time simply because of absorbed and manifested knowledge based on experience.

Perfect Your Pitch

What writers need to do is inquire of themselves whether they possess a special, potentially noticeable knowledge. Do you have private experiences of something that might interest millions of people? I'm not just talking about sensationalism à la Geraldo, but matters that you have actually encountered and which moved you. Check carefully whether you know of something that you can corner, as it were.

Extrapolating from my own experience and that of others, including those I interviewed in this book, I would say that it is most crucial to get something substantial written before you get too involved in finding out how, where and when to set about pitching. When you have something really good, be it a treatment, a script or a proposal, you usually know it. That is the time to get into marketing and thinking about the business end of the process.

After you've finished some creation and are satisfied that it accurately represents your thoughts and feelings about the subject matter, then go ahead and find the right broker to get it to the people who pay the money and distribute the goods. This is a cardinal rule of strong salesmanship—have something really good to sell. Even if you feel that the idea in your head is totally brilliant and without parallel in the television business, it is still vital to frame it in a form that TV people can understand.

This does not mean you should be a strict conformist in the content or style of your written or created piece. Artists, even those involved in the mercantile atmosphere of broadcast television, must always reach out to find new means of expression and communication. Just make sure that the people you are approaching do not get frightened away by a bizarre or lazy presentation. The more polished and professional the presentation, the more likely you are to get it produced. Pitching ultimately is like any other kind of salesmanship—you need a good product, you need to have researched your prospective buyers, and you need to economize your selling pitch, at every stage of the process.

As you complete this book, you should have a better idea of how to pitch and sell your writing. You need have your calling cards gathered at all times, whether you deliver them in the form of a query letter, a cover letter, a written treatment, or a live meeting. Everyone agrees that much can be observed by the buyer or broker-to-be from the way you open up your presentation. Sometimes writers feel that their exalted status obviates the need to perfect their pitch. If you want to compete in the television game, however, then you must get this part right. Think of yourself as a new kind of warrior, armed with good TV, maybe even revolutionary TV material. But first you must work your way into the hearts and minds of those in the industry. It is a real challenge, and it is better to perceive it as such so that you can keep getting better at it despite rejections and disappointments.

If you consider the pitching segment of your endeavor to be a subtle and demanding joust between you and the industry, then you may even learn to love the pitching a little, as tedious as it occasionally has to be. Bounce back, and don't take any single person's appraisal and decision as final or conclusive in any way unless that person can convince you you are wrong or at least a bit deluded about the quality and uniqueness of your work. And remember that some of the greatest works throughout the centuries met with chilly receptions. Stravinsky's work was resisted when it was first performed; some people thought the Beatles were trivial. Great art sometimes takes time to get through. Your television writing might just be ahead of its time, and you may be unable to break through until people catch up with it.

A New Era on the Horizon

New outlets, and old ones too for that matter, are always on the lookout for material. They need to fill up thousands of hours of television air time. Just take a look at any TV viewing guide and try and grasp how much air time there actually is to fill; it can't all be game shows and sports spectaculars. If you can think originally, if you're smart and prescient enough to imagine what the programmers will want at any given time, you will definitely prevail.

Agents need new clients, producers need new scripts, production companies need new supply contracts, studios and networks need new films. The demand for reality-based, quasi-documentary programming on television has also greatly increased. The American television marketplace is a voracious consumer of new product, and the place of the writer is central. This should be a source of optimism for you. The market should expand even further in the near future as cable TV penetrates more American households. This means that you stand a much better chance of getting your work on the air than did your colleagues of just ten years ago.

In the last decade of this century, the wild dreams of the seventies have been realized: Satellite television allows people living in the desert Southwest of the United States to pick up BBC dramas from the other side of the world; home video stores rent or sell practically any film from the entire history of the form; pay-per-view cable and basic cable networks are hungry for original programming to compete with the established networks and each other; venturing into filmmaking is less risky because of these expanded markets and computable, predictable ancillary profits. These are all very good for the new writer or television creator. There is more room for new drama and even more interest in good, nonfiction programming, which still needs good writers. Although it is obviously still a major triumph to get your work aired on television, it has never been easier.

As we reach the end of this century, the global communications industry is gaining in prominence, particularly as the old smoke-stack, industrial-based economies are taking a beating and the Japanese and Korean communications and computer industries are gaining in power and world influence. Thousands of hours of programming are needed to fill the new conduits across the planet, and the United States still leads easily in that department.

Once you have made a real commitment to writing television professionally, then I believe you will eventually prevail and make a living from your writing. Your progress may include rough periods or even times when you cannot believe you will ever receive acceptance and recognition, but it isn't too farfetched to say that if you are persevering and dedicated, your efforts will pay off and you will see your work on the screen.

So feel confident about the importance of your craft as we explore the growing horizons of television in the 1990s and beyond. I wish you the very best of luck in your writing career. I would also remind you, no matter what the commercial criteria, to create from your deepest and most perceptive imaginative space and to believe in the truth that every time something superior gets on the air, the whole population benefits.

Index

See also Backing
Public TV
    collaboration in, 110-111
    drama specials on, 42
    payment in, 109
    writing drama for, 101-102
    See also Doherty, Lynne
Publications, for industry
    reading, 84

Q

Quality
    of proposal, 11
    of work, 5
Query letter
    examples of, 23-24, 25-26
    to agents, 22-26, 145-146
Quiet Victory, 132

R

Rationale, for nonfiction
    proposal, 48-49
Reading
    about scriptwriting, 6, 92
    publications for, 84
Realism, in episodics, 32
Rejection, 13-14
    See also Criticism
Research, before submitting
    script, 106-108
Résumés, 69-70
Revision, 13-14
    radical, at producer's request,
        72-73
Rewards, of getting work
    produced, 8-9
Rights, acquiring, to story, 39
Rockefeller Foundation, 9, 56-57
Rothenberg, Randall, 151-152

S

Sample script, 34-35, 40-41
Script
    length of, 27

proper formatting of, 27
    sample, 34-35, 40-41
    submission of. *See* Submissions
Script, completed
    for TV movie, 40
    vs. treatment, 108-109
Scriptwriting, books about, 6
Serial. *See* Soap opera
Shows
    crime, 31-33
    fine arts, 66
    how-to, 65-66
    importance of studying, 34
    magazine, 45-46
    nature, 65
Siberell, Brian, 135-150
Simon, Ronni, 89-100
Sitcom
    breaking into, 35-37, 92
    inventing new, 36
Sitcom writers, passion of, 10
Situation comedy. *See* Sitcom
Soap operas, 41-42
    prime time, 33-34
Spec script. *See* Writing, on spec
Sponsorship, corporate
    history of, 121-122
    in cable TV, 124-125
Staff job, on news magazine,
    64-65
Stand and Deliver, 117-119
Story
    acquiring rights to, 39
    personal, new writer and,
        105-106
Streisand, Barbra, and Ronni
    Simon, 94
Subject matter
    controversial, 130, 139
    for TV movie, 38-40
    social issues as, 129-130, 134
    writer's interest in, 5-6, 9
Submission guidelines, for

U

OTHER BOOKS OF INTEREST

Annual Market Books
  Children's Writer's & Illustrator's Market, edited by Lisa Carpenter (paper) $16.95
  Novel & Short Story Writer's Market, edited by Robin Gee (paper) $18.95
  Photographer's Market, edited by Sam Marshall $21.95
  Writer's Market, edited by Mark Kissling $24.95
General Writing Books
  Annable's Treasury of Literary Teasers, by H.D. Annable (paper) $10.95
  Beginning Writer's Answer Book, edited by Kirk Polking (paper) $13.95
  Discovering the Writer Within, by Bruce Ballenger & Barry Lane $16.95
  Getting the Words Right: How to Rewrite, Edit and Revise, by Theodore A. Rees Cheney (paper) $12.95
  How to Write a Book Proposal, by Michael Larsen (paper) $10.95
  Just Open a Vein, edited by William Brohaugh $15.95
  Knowing Where to Look: The Ultimate Guide to Research, by Lois Horowitz (paper) $15.95
  Make Your Words Work, by Gary Provost $17.95
  On Being a Writer, edited by Bill Strickland $19.95
  Pinckert's Practical Grammar, by Robert C. Pinckert (paper) $11.95
  The Story Behind the Word, by Morton S. Freeman (paper) $9.95
  12 Keys to Writing Books That Sell, by Kathleen Krull (paper) $12.95
  The 29 Most Common Writing Mistakes & How to Avoid Them, by Judy Delton (paper) $9.95
  The Wordwatcher's Guide to Good Writing & Grammar, by Morton S. Freeman (paper) $15.95
  Word Processing Secrets for Writers, by Michael A. Banks & Ansen Dibell (paper) $14.95
  The Writer's Book of Checklists, by Scott Edelstein $16.95
  The Writer's Digest Guide to Manuscript Formats, by Buchman & Groves $17.95
Nonfiction Writing
  The Complete Guide to Writing Biographies, by Ted Schwarz $19.95
  Creative Conversations: The Writer's Guide to Conducting Interviews, by Michael Schumacher $16.95
  How to Sell Every Magazine Article You Write, by Lisa Collier Cool (paper) $11.95
  How to Write Irresistible Query Letters, by Lisa Collier Cool (paper) $10.95
  The Writer's Digest Handbook of Magazine Article Writing, edited by Jean M. Fredette (paper) $11.95
Fiction Writing
  The Art & Craft of Novel Writing, by Oakley Hall $17.95
  Best Stories from New Writers, edited by Linda Sanders $16.95
  Characters & Viewpoint, by Orson Scott Card $13.95
  The Complete Guide to Writing Fiction, by Barnaby Conrad $17.95
  Cosmic Critiques: How & Why 10 Science Fiction Stories Work, edited by Asimov & Greenberg (paper) $12.95
  Creating Characters: How to Build Story People, by Dwight V. Swain $16.95
  Creating Short Fiction, by Damon Knight (paper) $10.95
  Dare to Be a Great Writer: 329 Keys to Powerful Fiction, by Leonard Bishop $16.95
  Dialogue, by Lewis Turco $13.95
  Handbook of Short Story Writing: Vol. I, by Dickson and Smythe (paper) $9.95
  How to Write & Sell Your First Novel, by Collier & Leighton (paper) $12.95
  Manuscript Submission, by Scott Edelstein $13.95
  Plot, by Ansen Dibell $13.95

Revision, by Kit Reed $13.95
Spider Spin Me a Web: Lawrence Block on Writing Fiction, by Lawrence Block $16.95
Theme & Strategy, by Ronald B. Tobias $13.95
Writing the Novel: From Plot to Print, by Lawrence Block (paper) $10.95

Special Interest Writing Books

Armed & Dangerous: A Writer's Guide to Weapons, by Michael Newton (paper) $14.95
The Complete Book of Scriptwriting, by J. Michael Straczynski (paper) $11.95
Deadly Doses: A Writer's Guide to Poisons, by Serita Deborah Stevens with Anne Klarner (paper) $16.95
Hillary Waugh's Guide to Mysteries & Mystery Writing, by Hillary Waugh $19.95
How to Write a Play, by Raymond Hull (paper) $12.95
How to Write Action/Adventure Novels, by Michael Newton $13.95
How to Write & Sell True Crime, by Gary Provost $17.95
How to Write Horror Fiction, by William F. Nolan $15.95
How to Write Mysteries, by Shannon OCork $13.95
How to Write Romances, by Phyllis Taylor Pianka $13.95
How to Write Science Fiction & Fantasy, by Orson Scott Card $13.95
How to Write the Story of Your Life, by Frank P. Thomas (paper) $11.95
How to Write Western Novels, by Matt Braun $13.95
The Magazine Article: How To Think It, Plan It, Write It, by Peter Jacobi $17.95
Mystery Writer's Handbook, by The Mystery Writers of America (paper) $11.95
Successful Scriptwriting, by Jurgen Wolff & Kerry Cox (paper) $14.95
TV Scriptwriter's Handbook, by Alfred Brenner (paper) $10.95
The Writer's Complete Crime Reference Book, by Martin Roth $19.95
Writing for Children & Teenagers, 3rd Edition, by Lee Wyndham & Arnold Madison (paper) $12.95
Writing the Modern Mystery, by Barbara Norville $15.95

The Writing Business

A Beginner's Guide to Getting Published, edited by Kirk Polking (paper) $11.95
The Complete Guide to Self-Publishing, by Tom & Marilyn Ross (paper) $16.95
How to Write with a Collaborator, by Hal Bennett with Michael Larsen $11.95
How You Can Make $25,000 a Year Writing, by Nancy Edmonds Hanson (paper) $12.95
Time Management for Writers, by Ted Schwarz $10.95
The Writer's Friendly Legal Guide, edited by Kirk Polking $16.95
Writer's Guide to Self-Promotion & Publicity, by Elane Feldman $16.95
A Writer's Guide to Contract Negotiations, by Richard Balkin (paper) $11.95
Writing A to Z, edited by Kirk Polking $22.95

To order directly from the publisher, include $3.00 postage and handling for 1 book and $1.00 for each additional book. Allow 30 days for delivery.

Writer's Digest Books
1507 Dana Avenue, Cincinnati, Ohio 45207
Credit card orders call TOLL-FREE
1-800-289-0963
Prices subject to change without notice.

Write to this same address for information on *Writer's Digest* magazine, *Story* magazine, Writer's Digest Book Club, Writer's Digest School, and Writer's Digest Criticism Service.